Past Masters
General Editor Keith Thomas

Freud

Anthony Storr qualified as a doctor in 1944. He
subsequently specialized in psychiatry, trained as an
analyst, and taught psychotherapy at Oxford. His
previous books include *The Integrity of the
Personality* (1960), *The Dynamics of Creation* (1972),
Jung (Modern Masters, 1973), *Solitude* (1988), and
Music and the Mind (1992). He is an Emeritus Fellow
of Green College, Oxford.

Past Masters

Forthcoming

Anthony Storr

Freud

Oxford   New York
OXFORD UNIVERSITY PRESS

Oxford University Press, Walton Street, Oxford OX2 6DP

Oxford New York
Athens Auckland Bangkok Bombay
Calcutta Cape Town Dar es Salaam Delhi
Florence Hong Kong Istanbul Karachi
Kuala Lumpur Madras Madrid Melbourne
Mexico City Nairobi Paris Singapore
Taipei Tokyo Toronto

and associated companies in
Berlin Ibadan

Oxford is a trade mark of Oxford University Press

First published 1989 as an Oxford University Press paperback
Reissued 1996

British Library Cataloguing in Publication Data
Data available

Library of Congress Cataloging in Publication Data
Storr, Anthony.
Freud/Anthony Storr.
p.   cm.—(Past masters)
Bibliography: Includes index.
1. Psychoanalysis.   2. Freud, Sigmund, 1856–1939.
I. Title.   II. Series.
150.19'52—dc19   BF173.S836   1989   88-25407
ISBN 0–19–282210–1 (pbk.)

10 9

Printed in Great Britain by
Biddles Ltd
Guildford and King's Lynn

Acknowledgements

Sir Keith Thomas made valuable comments on the text, and Catherine Clarke has proved an expert editor. I am particularly grateful to Dr Charles Rycroft, who drew my attention to some omissions, and made other useful suggestions. I owe a considerable debt to his books, as well as to his critical appraisal of the present text.

Contents

1 Life and character

Sigmund Freud was born on 6 May 1856 in the Moravian town of Freiberg, now Pribor in Czechoslovakia. His mother Amalie was the third wife of Jacob Freud, a Jewish wool merchant, some twenty years younger than her husband. In 1859, when Sigmund Freud was 3 years old, the family moved to Vienna. For the next seventy-nine years Freud continued to live and work in this city, for which he recurrently professed distaste, but which he was extremely reluctant to leave. In 1938, he was compelled to take refuge from the Nazis, and spent the last year of his life in England, dying on 23 September 1939, shortly after the beginning of the Second World War.

Freud's mother, a vivacious and charming lady who survived until the age of 95, was only 21 when Freud was born. She went on to bear seven other children; but Sigmund, referred to by her as 'mein goldener Sigi', remained her indisputable favourite, one circumstance to which Freud attributed his inner confidence. Freud also believed that his later success was directly related to his being a Jew. Although Freud never practised the Jewish religion and dismissed all religious belief as illusory, he was very conscious of being Jewish, made few friends who were not Jews, regularly attended the meetings of B'nai B'rith, his local Jewish society, and declined royalties from those of his books which were translated into Yiddish and Hebrew. He attributed his intellectual autonomy to his being Jewish, writing that, when he first encountered anti-Semitism at the University of Vienna, his lack of acceptance by the community drove him into opposition and fostered his independence of judgement.

As a boy, Freud was intellectually precocious and an extremely hard worker. For six successive years, Freud was first in his class at school; and, by the time he left, had not only obtained a thorough knowledge of Greek, Latin, German and Hebrew, but had learned French and English, and had also

1

taught himself the rudiments of Spanish and Italian. He began to read Shakespeare at the age of 8. Shakespeare and Goethe remained his favourite authors. From his earliest years, Freud was a serious, dedicated student who was evidently expected by his family and teachers to make his mark in the world, and who himself acquired a conviction that he was destined to make some important contribution to knowledge. Family life revolved around his studies. He took his evening meal apart from the rest of the family and, because the sound of her practising disturbed him, his sister Anna's piano was removed from the apartment by his parents.

Freud enrolled in the medical department of the University of Vienna in the autumn of 1873, but did not graduate until 30 March 1881. His initial interest was in zoological research. From 1876 to 1882 he carried out research in the Physiological Institute of Ernst Brücke, an authority whom he greatly admired and who exercised a considerable influence upon his thinking. Brücke and his co-workers were dedicated to the idea, then not widely accepted, that all vital processes could ultimately be explained in terms of physics and chemistry, thus eliminating religious and vitalist concepts from biology. Freud remained a determinist throughout his life, believing that all vital phenomena, including psychological phenomena like thoughts, feelings and phantasies, are rigidly determined by the principle of cause and effect.

Freud was reluctant to practise medicine, and would have been content to spend his life in research. But, in 1882, he fell in love and became engaged to Martha Bernays. Since there was no possibility of his earning enough to support a wife and family if he remained in Brücke's laboratory, Freud reluctantly abandoned his research career, and spent the next three years gaining medical experience in the Vienna General Hospital, preparatory to embarking upon medical practice. In 1885 he was appointed a lecturer in neuropathology at the University of Vienna. From October 1885 to February 1886 he worked at the Salpêtrière Hospital in Paris under the great neurologist Charcot, whose teaching on hysteria awoke his interest in the problems of the neuroses, as opposed to organic diseases of the nervous system. In April 1886 Freud opened his medical practice in Vienna, and, on 13 September, at last married his fiancée.

Their first child, Mathilde, was born in October 1887. Five more children were to follow; the last being Anna Freud, born in 1895, the only one of Freud's children to become a psycho-analyst. His wife Martha was content to devote herself entirely to his welfare and to that of their six children throughout their long and tranquil married life. We know from letters that their sexual life declined comparatively early; but their family life remained harmonious. After his death, she wrote to a friend:

> And yet how terribly difficult it is to have to do without him. To continue to live without so much kindness and wisdom beside one! It is small comfort for me to know that in the fifty-three years of our married life not one angry word fell between us and that I always sought as much as possible to remove from his path the misery of everyday life.

From the mid-1890s onward, Freud's life becomes the history of the development of psycho-analysis. *Studies on Hysteria*, written jointly with Josef Breuer, appeared in 1895. If one considers the influence which Freud has had upon contemporary thought, and the fact that his own contributions to psycho-analysis are so extensive as to require twenty-four volumes, it is extraordinary that the first psycho-analytic publication did not appear until he was 39 years old.

What kind of personality is able to achieve so much within the span of only half a lifetime? Most people of outstanding intellectual achievement exhibit traits of personality which psychiatrists label obsessional; that is, they are meticulous, scrupulous, accurate, reliable, honest, and much concerned with cleanliness, control and order. Only when these admirable traits become exaggerated do we speak of obsessional neurosis, a disorder which ranges in severity from mild compulsions to check and re-check to a state of total disablement in which the sufferer's existence is so dominated by rituals that normal life becomes impossible.

Freud himself recognized that his personality was obsessional, and told Jung that, if he were to suffer from neurosis, it would be of the obsessional type. His intellectual precocity, and his dedication to work, which remained compulsive from boyhood onwards, are characteristic. He wrote to his friend Fliess that he needed a 'dominating passion'. He claimed that he could not contemplate a life without work, and that, for him, the creative imagination and work went together. He was an enormously productive writer. Most of his writing was done on Sundays, or late at night after a day in which he might have spent eight or nine demanding hours seeing analytic patients. Although he took long summer holidays, during which he was an energetic walker, he allowed himself little time for relaxation during the working week.

Like most people with this type of personality, Freud was extremely neat in dress and appearance, even when early poverty made this difficult. A letter to Wilhelm Fliess reveals that a barber attended him daily. He exhibited all the most valuable traits characteristic of this variety of personality, being scrupulous, self-controlled, honest and passionately concerned with the pursuit of truth. Freud himself described obsessional personalities as being 'especially *orderly*, *parsimonious* and *obstinate*' (*SE*, IX.169). He was certainly orderly and obstinate; and may have appeared parsimonious in his early days, when he was extremely poor and dependent on the financial help of friends like Josef Breuer. His tastes remained simple, and Ernest Jones tells us that he never owned more than three suits, three pairs of shoes, and three sets of underclothes. In later years, he could not tolerate owing money to anyone; and, although charging high fees to those who could afford them, gave generous financial help to those in need, including some patients, his own relatives, and poverty-stricken students.

He also suffered from some of the tensions which are inseparable from the valuable traits found in obsessional personalities. He was superstitious about numbers. In a letter to Jung (16 April 1909), he reveals that, for many years, he was convinced that he would die between the ages of 61 and 62. In 1904, he went to Greece with his brother, and writes that it was 'really uncanny' how often the number 61 or 60 kept on cropping up in connection with 1 or 2. His hotel room in Athens was numbered 31; that is, half of 62. He tells Jung that this obsession first appeared in 1899.

> At that time two events occurred. First, I wrote 'The Inter-pretation of Dreams' (which appeared postdated 1900), second, I received a new telephone number which I still have today: 14362. It is easy to find a factor common to these two events. In 1899 when I wrote 'The Interpretation of Dreams' I was 43 years old. Thus it was plausible to suppose that the other figures signified the end of my life, hence 61 or 62 (*The Freud-Jung Letters*, 219).

Such superstitions, often combined with compulsive rituals and with a preoccupation with death, are commonly found in cases of obsessional neurosis. Ernest Jones has drawn attention to the fact that, like many other creative men of genius, Freud exhibited a peculiar oscillation between scepticism and credulity. Although Freud did not subscribe to the belief in mediums and 'spiritualism' which seduced so many scientists towards the end of the nineteenth century, he did retain an irrational conviction about the occult significance of numbers and a more than half-hearted belief in telepathy.

Freud exhibited a number of other obsessional habits and traits. For example, he was a compulsive smoker of cigars. When, during the years 1893 to 1896, he suffered from a recurrent cardiac arrhythmia which may have been partly attributable to smoking, he found it impossible to abstain for long. At the age of 67, he developed a cancerous condition of the palate which recurred throughout the rest of his life, requiring more than thirty operations. Although he knew that smoking was an agent which provoked recurrence by the irritation which it caused, he was unable to abandon the habit. Obsessional personalities usually exhibit self-control to the point of appearing inhibited and lacking in spontaneity, and Freud was no exception. But smoking was his Achilles' heel; a compulsive part of his behaviour which he was unable to master.

5

His collecting habits were also characteristic. Freud had a passion for antiquities, stimulated by his classical studies, his romantic longing for Rome, and his interest in the remoter aspects of human history. Photographs of his apartment in Vienna, and the reconstruction of that apartment in his study at 20 Maresfield Gardens, Hampstead, now the Freud Museum, show his collection of antique statuettes. These crowd the shelves and the top of his desk so closely that not one can be appreciated as an aesthetic object in its own right. This display is not that of a connoisseur but that of an obsessional collector whose interest is in accumulation rather than in beauty. Freud himself realized that his interest in such objects, like his interest in sculpture, depended upon the historical associations of the object and its emotional and intellectual meaning rather than upon its aesthetic form. He frankly admits as much in his essay on 'The Moses of Michelangelo'; a piece which also exhibits Freud's meticulous attention to small details which would escape the scrutiny of most observers. This close attention to detail also showed itself in his clinical interpretations of his patients' symptoms, dreams, and other psychological material.

Freud had a lively appreciation of literature. The excellence of Freud's own literary style was recognized when he was still a schoolboy. In 1930, he became the fourth recipient of the Goethe prize for literature awarded by the City of Frankfurt. In Freud's collected works there are more references to Goethe and to Shakespeare than there are to the writings of any psychiatrist. His appreciation of music was confined to opera, the type of musical performance which most appeals to the unmusical. A nephew describes him as despising music.

Freud's inhibited, controlled nature extended to his autobiography, which concentrates almost entirely upon the development of psycho-analysis and tells us next to nothing about his personal life. As early as 1885, he wrote to his fiancée telling her that he had destroyed his notes, letters and manuscripts of the last fourteen years, presciently adding that he had no desire to make it easy for his future biographers. Freud, the man who spent his life investigating the kind of intimate secrets which people strive to conceal from themselves as well as from others, was extremely reluctant to reveal his own.

In his clinical work, Freud was kind and tolerant, as psycho-analysts have to be. However, his kindness was not based upon any great expectations of the human race, whom he regarded with distaste or with detachment rather than with love.

> I have found little that is 'good' about human beings on the whole. In my experience, most of them are trash . . .
> *(Psychoanalysis and Faith*, 61–2)

he wrote in one letter.

One analysand records that his interest was

> curiously impersonal . . . He was so concentrated on the inquiry he was pursuing that his self functioned only as an instrument.

Those who were close to him admired him, not only for his intelligence and breadth of culture, but also for his integrity and courage. Perhaps he lacked something in immediate warmth. In a letter to Jung (2 September 1907) Freud wrote:

> I have always felt that there is something about my per-sonality, my ideas and manner of speaking, that people find strange and repellent, whereas all hearts open to you. If a healthy man like you regards himself as an hysterical type, I can only claim for myself the 'obsessional' type, each specimen of which vegetates in a sealed-off world of his own.
> *(The Freud-Jung Letters*, 82)

Freud's honesty compelled him substantially to modify or revise his ideas on a number of occasions throughout his long life; but this always seems to have been brought about by new insights of his own rather than by any response to the criticism of others. When Freud had reached a particular conclusion, he was intolerant of disagreement, and this rigidity led to the long series of defections among his collaborators and disciples which is such a regrettable feature of psycho-analytic history.

Freud treated such defections as betrayals rather than as intellectual divergences. Breuer, the first collaborator to become estranged, wrote to Forel:

> Freud is a man given to absolute and exclusive formulations: this is a psychical need which, in my opinion, leads to excessive generalization.

Breuer was right on both counts. Where human frailty was concerned, Freud exhibited a quite unusual tolerance. This, because it has led to a more civilized attitude towards neurosis, sexual deviation and other forms of emotional maladaptation, is one of Freud's most valuable legacies. But, in the early days of psycho-analysis, he could not allow those close to him to dispute what he claimed to be the fundamental, absolute tenets of the new science of the mind which he had originated; and this led not only to the breaches with Breuer and Fliess, but to the departure of Adler, Stekel, Jung, Rank, and others from the psycho-analytic movement.

Breuer's remark about 'excessive generalization' is also well founded. Freud was a bold and original thinker; but the nature and length of the psycho-analytic procedure which he invented meant that he based his conclusions about human nature on a very small sample of the human race. Freud's patients belonged predominantly to the upper or upper-middle classes. More-over, the type of case upon which early psycho-analytic theory was originally based, namely, severe conversion hysteria in women, is seldom seen today.

Excessive generalization is a temptation for all original thinkers, who are usually in love with their own ideas and who therefore over-value them. Perhaps novel and unpopular ideas would never win a hearing unless their originators were entirely convinced that they were right. Freud was not only sure that he had discovered new aspects of the truth about human beings, but he was also a persuasive writer who endeavoured to meet all possible criticisms which his readers might advance in the course of his own exposition; a technique which is deliberately 'disarming'. He expected hostility and incredulity and often experienced both. But his literary skill and his absolute conviction of his own rightness eventually made psycho-analysis a force to be reckoned with throughout the Western world.

There is also another reason for over-generalization which springs not from over-valuation of the new ideas, but from a desire or need which is very characteristic of thinkers with obsessional personalities. Because their psychology is based on the need to order and control, they tend to look for, and be attracted by, comprehensive systems of thought which promise near-complete explanations of human existence, and which therefore hold out the hope that the individual can master both his own nature and external reality by means of his new understanding. Many of the greatest philosophers, including Kant and Wittgenstein, were people of this kind, creating their own systems, impervious to the ideas of others, often unable to read the works of other philosophers with profit or pleasure.

Freud claimed to be a scientist, and was certainly not a philosopher in the technical sense, nor particularly interested in the subject, although, as a young man, he had translated a book by John Stuart Mill. Nevertheless, he resembled some philosophers in being a system-builder. Very early in its history, psycho-analysis left the narrow confines of the consulting room and made incursions into anthropology, sociology, religion, literature, art, and the occult. It became, if not a philosophical system, at least a *Weltanschauung*; and this extraordinary expansion of a method of treating neurotics into a new way of regarding human nature had its origin in the psychological needs of its founder. Freud repudiated religion as an illusion, yet needed some systematic approach to making coherent sense out of the world. He called the system which he invented a science; but psycho-analysis is not, and could never have been, a science in the sense in which physics or chemistry are sciences, since its hypotheses are retrospective and cannot be used for prediction, and most are insusceptible of final proof. Freud's deterministic stance, and his insistence that psycho-analysis was a science, have discredited his discoveries in the eyes of philosophers like Popper, and of scientists like

Medawar, with the consequence that they have failed to appreciate the importance of psycho-analysis as a hermeneutic system and as a way of looking at human nature. A short book cannot attempt an account of everything that Freud wrote. What follows is an attempt to evaluate his more important theories in the light of modern knowledge.

2 From trauma to phantasy

Freud's brief sojourn in Paris during the winter of 1885–6 had a profound effect upon his thinking. Charcot had, for some years, been investigating hypnosis, with the object of discovering a diagnostic technique which would distinguish between paralyses which were the consequence of organic disease of the central nervous system and paralyses which were hysterical, that is, 'neurotic' in origin. Charcot demonstrated to Freud that *ideas*, although intangible, could nevertheless be causal agents in neurosis. When a patient developed a hysterical paralysis, the form which the paralysis took was not determined by the facts of anatomy, but by the patient's faulty *idea* of anatomy. Instead of developing a paralysis which could be explained by a lesion of a particular peripheral nerve, he exhibited a paralysis of a limb which corresponded to his idea of where his leg or arm began and ended. Charcot demonstrated that such paralyses could be cured, and then artificially produced again, by hypnotic suggestion.

Freud learned from Charcot that, in order to understand hysteria, he had to look to psychology rather than to neurology. Since patients awaking from the trance-like state induced by hypnosis could not recall what had been suggested to them whilst hypnotized, hypnotic experiments also taught Freud that mental processes which took place unconsciously could have a powerful effect upon behaviour.

Freud therefore employed hypnosis in the treatment of neurotic patients and continued to do so until 1896. But he did not use hypnosis solely as a means of implanting suggestions of positive health. A second and more important aspect derived from the observations of Freud's friend and colleague, Josef Breuer. When treating his famous case, Anna O. (Bertha Pappenheim), with hypnosis, Breuer discovered that, if she could recall the first moment at which a particular hysterical symptom appeared, and re-experience the emotion accompanying this, the symptom disappeared. Breuer named this method of treatment 'catharsis'. Hypnosis, therefore, came to be used as a method of enabling the patient to recall the forgotten origins of particular symptoms. Instead of being used as a direct attack upon symptoms by means of suggestion, it became a method of investigation.

Freud and Breuer came to hope that all neurotic symptoms could be abolished in this laborious, though essentially simple way. In their first paper in *Studies on Hysteria*, they wrote:

> For we found, to our great surprise at first, that *each individual hysterical symptom immediately and permanently disappeared when we had succeeded in bringing clearly to light the memory of the event by which it was provoked and in arousing the accompanying affect, and when the patient had described that event in the greatest possible detail and had put the affect into words.*

In a famous sentence, Breuer and Freud proclaimed:

Hysterics suffer mainly from reminiscences (*SE*, II.6, 7).

These reminiscences were of a special kind. First, they were not easily accessible to conscious recall. The patient could only recover them if hypnotized or if, as Freud later discovered, the patient was authoritatively told that the memories were there, could certainly be retrieved, and would return at the moment when the physician pressed the patient's forehead with his hand. Second, the reminiscences were invariably painful, shameful, or alarming. It followed that there must be some mental mechanism which tended to banish unpleasant memories from consciousness and make them relatively inaccessible. This mechanism Freud named *repression*; and repression, the first 'mechanism of defence', became the corner-stone of the psycho-analytic theory of neurosis. Already, he was postulating the existence of *conflict* within the mind; conflict between some emotion (affect) which was seeking to become conscious and to be discharged, and another part of the mind which refused to admit or face the existence of an emotion which it found repellent.

Freud postulated that the disowned affect which had become repressed, being unable to find direct expression and discharge, gave rise to neurotic symptoms. The mental state which Freud proposed is analogous to the physical condition of a 'blind' boil or abscess which, being unable to find a path to the surface of the body, cannot discharge the toxic matter which it contains. This 'surgical' view of neurosis is one which must have appealed to Freud as a medical scientist. It implied that the disowned affect which was causing the neurotic symptoms could be excised as if it were a foreign body; an intruder which was not part of the patient's personality as a whole.

In a case of hysteria, Freud affirmed that the affect became converted into a physical symptom; hence the term 'conversion hysteria'. In many instances, the physical symptom expressed the patient's feelings in symbolic fashion. Thus, constriction in the throat might express an inability to swallow an insult; or a pain in the region of the heart might signify that the patient's heart had been metaphorically broken or damaged. In other types of neurosis, a variety of neurotic symptoms, like obsessions and phobias, resulted from the repressed affect struggling to express itself indirectly.

At first, Freud thought of the repressed affect as being always associated with trauma; that is, with some unpleasant event which the patient wished to forget. This observation is still valid today in cases of so-called 'traumatic neurosis', in which a patient has developed neurotic symptoms following a near escape from death, an accident, or some horrific experience like being tortured. Enabling such a patient to recover the memory of the experience, to go through it in detail, and to discharge or 'abreact' the emotions of fear and horror which accompanied the experience does indeed have beneficial results, as those who treated wartime neuroses have repeatedly demonstrated.

Later, Freud extended the notion to include instinctual impulses seeking discharge which might either be aroused by some external stimulus, or might simply arise spontaneously within the person. An early example which illustrates this is the case of a girl who found it impossible to leave her room or

13

receive visitors without having urinated a number of times. Freud traced the origin of the symptom to an occasion on which the girl had been in a theatre and had found herself so strongly attracted by a particular man that she had experienced genital sensations which had led to her wanting to urinate and to being compelled to leave the theatre. Since that occasion, she had feared a repetition of the sensation, and had replaced the fear of her erotic impulses with a fear of being unable to control her bladder. Recovery of the memory of the origin of her symptom together with, one may suppose, recognition and acceptance of her sexuality, effected a cure.

At this time, Freud also proposed that there was a special group of neuroses which were directly caused by unsatisfactory or incomplete discharge of sexual impulses. Such incomplete discharge was brought about by practices like masturbation or *coitus interruptus*, or simply by sexual abstinence. Freud called such states 'actual neuroses', from the German *aktuelle*, meaning 'current'. Substitution of normal sexual activity for the previous practice was enough to cure such cases.

Even at this very early stage in the development of psychoanalysis, one can recognize certain ideas which were to influence Freud throughout the rest of his life. The first is that, except in the cases of 'actual neurosis', past emotions are the cause of present problems; the second, that such emotions are invariably shameful or painful or frightening, and therefore repudiated and repressed. Freud always believed that a dominating principle of mental life was the need of the organism to reach a state of tranquillity by completely discharging all tensions (this was later named the Nirvana principle). This basic assumption tends to treat all powerful emotions in a negative fashion, as disturbances which must be got rid of, rather than as pleasures to be sought. Bliss, in the Freudian scheme, is attained when needs have been satisfied and passions spent. There is no place for 'stimulus hunger', the need which human beings have to seek out emotional and intellectual stimuli when they are placed in a monotonous environment with little input from the outside world, or when they have been in a state of tranquillity for so long that they suffer from *ennui*.

Freud's next step was to assert that, in many cases of hysteria, the trauma which ostensibly provoked the onset of symptoms was often too trivial to be an adequate determinant. In such cases, Freud alleged, the ostensible trauma had awoken memories of an earlier trauma, and it was this combination of present with past trauma which constituted the true provocation. In an early paper, based on a lecture which he delivered in Vienna in 1896, Freud affirmed that:

> *no hysterical symptom can arise from a real experience alone, but that in every case the memory of earlier experiences awakened in association to it plays a part in causing the symptom* (*SE*, III.197).

Freud then made a momentous statement. On the basis of eighteen cases of hysteria he asserted:

> Whatever case and whatever symptom we take as our point of departure, *in the end we infallibly come to the field of sexual experience* (*SE*, III.199).

In the same paper, Freud continues:

> I therefore put forward the thesis that at the bottom of every case of hysteria there are *one or more occurrences of pre-mature sexual experience*, occurrences which belong to the earliest years of childhood but which can be reproduced through the work of psycho-analysis in spite of the intervening decades. I believe that this is an important finding, the discovery of a *caput Nili* in neuropathology (*SE*, III.203).

Roger Brown, a professor of psychology at Harvard, has drawn attention to the fact that this was Freud's last attempt to give figures concerning aetiology, and that, even in this instance, there were no controls. In spite of this, Freud continued to claim that he was a scientist.

Freud's findings made sexual emotions the key emotions which, if repressed, were the cause of neurotic symptoms.

15

Although he recognized that other emotions could be implicated in hysterical symptoms, for example, resentment at an insult which could not be 'swallowed' causing constriction in the throat, sexuality, rather than aggression, became Freud's central preoccupation and remained so for many years. The popular perception that psycho-analysis is chiefly concerned with sex is largely justified, although there is a good deal more to psycho-analysis than popular perception recognizes. For Freud, sex was especially suitable as a linchpin around which psycho-analytic theory could circle and coalesce. For sex not only gives rise to powerful emotions which are often repudiated and therefore repressed, but it also bridges the gap between mind and body, in that it is responsible for a great many purely psychological manifestations like thoughts, phantasies, and dreams, and yet is obviously physical, both in its hormonal origin and in its ultimate expression. Freud, faithful to his training in Brücke's laboratories, continued to hope that neurosis could ultimately be shown to be physical in origin, although he had abandoned his own attempt to link neurotic mechanisms with cerebral anatomy and physiology (the so-called 'Project for a Scientific Psychology') by 1897. In a letter to Jung dated 19 April 1908, he wrote:

> In the sexual processes we have the indispensable 'organic foundation' without which a medical man can only feel ill at ease in the life of the psyche (*The Freud-Jung Letters*, 140–1).

Freud became more and more convinced that the chief characteristic of the neurotic person was lack of a normal sex life and that sexual satisfaction was the key to happiness. This implied that the healthy person was fully able to discharge the tensions caused by his sexual impulses in repeated, satisfying orgasm, thus recurrently experiencing the state of tensionless Nirvana referred to above.

Freud at first concluded that, in cases of hysteria, the premature sexual experience which constituted the core of the neurosis in early childhood was seduction of the child by an adult. This was often seduction of a daughter by a father, as in the case of Katharina, which Freud described in *Studies on Hysteria*, though originally disguising 'father' as 'uncle'. Freud realized that not all those who had been seduced as children became neurotic; but maintained that this was because they had retained *conscious* access to the traumatic experience, whereas those who later became neurotic had repressed it. Freud's tendency to generalization made him conclude that all his patients had suffered sexual seduction in early childhood, a conclusion which, in a number of instances, his patients were eager to confirm, but which, as Freud himself realized, he might have forced on them because of the strength of his own conviction.

There were three reasons for Freud's subsequent abandonment of the seduction theory. The first was that, although sexual seduction of young children by adults undoubtedly occurred, Freud could not believe that this happened quite so frequently as his growing practice suggested. The second was that, if actual seduction was an invariable precursor to the development of hysterical symptoms, Freud would have been forced to conclude that his own father had been guilty of such acts, since he had noted the existence of some hysterical symptoms in his brother and sisters. The third reason was that, in the course of his own self-analysis, Freud had become more and more impressed with the importance of sexual phantasy. He had, for example, recognized that in his own early childhood he had experienced erotic feelings towards his mother when he saw her naked. He concluded that many of his patients were recounting sexual phantasies of being seduced by a parent rather than recalling actual events.

This was a significant change in Freud's thinking. As he put it himself, it led to the conclusion

that the neurotic symptoms were not related directly to actual events but to wishful phantasies, and that as far as the neurosis was concerned psychical reality was of more importance than material reality (*SE*, XX.34).

From this time onward, psycho-analysis changed from being an attempt to disclose a causal series of events culminating in the outbreak of a neurosis to an exploration of the patient's imaginative world, especially as that world manifested itself in the early years of childhood. The medical model of neurosis had almost disappeared, although Freud still believed that symptoms were related to the 'damming-up' of sexual tensions which were not properly discharged.

To face the collapse of a hypothesis so painstakingly constructed is daunting, and Freud's abandonment of the seduction theory was originally hailed as an example of his integrity and his uncompromising adherence to truth. J. M. Masson, editor and translator of Freud's letters to Fliess, has questioned Freud's honesty in a book in which he claims that Freud deliberately suppressed his findings about the sexual seduction of children in order not to outrage psychiatric opinion more than he had done already. This is so out of character with what we know of Freud's personality from those who were close to him that Masson's accusations can be dismissed. Nevertheless, in recent years, psychatrists and others have realized that sexual seduction of children is far more prevalent than they had hitherto supposed; and although such seduction is not necessarily followed by the development of hysterical symptoms in the way that Freud originally postulated, it does often have dire consequences for the subsequent emotional adjustment of the individual concerned.

It is quite possible that psycho-analysts have underestimated the occurrence of actual sexual seduction, and that they have treated as phantasies memories recalled by their patients which were accurate reports of real events. No one knows the actual prevalence of sexual seduction in childhood; but there is no doubt that increasing public tolerance of discussion of such matters, and the provision of facilities for children to report sexual abuse privately to understanding adults outside the family, has brought to light a great many cases which had previously been unreported.

Concentration upon the patient's inner world of phantasy has sometimes caused psycho-analysts to neglect, not only sexual seduction, but other real events and circumstances which influence people's lives. As we shall see, this is one of the criticisms levelled at 'classical' psycho-analysis by such critics as John Bowlby. But Freud's realization of the importance of phantasy is a corner-stone in the construction of psycho-analytic theory. He came to see that what was subjected to repression was not usually the memories of actual traumatic incidents (though these might certainly occur), but instinctual impulses manifesting themselves as phantasies. On this basis rest Freud's theories of infantile sexuality and libidinal development, and also his view of dreams.

3 Exploring the past

Infantile sexual development

Freud's rejection of the seduction theory did not shake his conviction that neurosis was connected with disturbances of the sexual function, nor his belief that neurosis originated in the earliest years of childhood. But instead of continuing to concentrate his attention upon traumatic incidents, he turned to studying the sexual and emotional development of children, and advanced the idea that neurosis in later life came about because the child's sexual development had been partly arrested at some immature stage. As he himself put it:

> A formula begins to take shape which lays it down that the sexuality of neurotics has remained in, or been brought back to, an infantile state (*SE*, VII.172).

In line with his requirement that psychological processes should, wherever possible, be formulated in terms of their 'indispensable organic foundation'. Freud couched his stages of infantile sexual development in terms of parts of the body rather than in terms of perception, cognition, learning, or attachment. During the first year of life, the infant's capacity for physical gratification is centred upon the mouth; this is the 'oral' stage. From around 1 to 3 years old, the anal region takes over. This is followed by the 'phallic' stage, in which the penis or clitoris becomes the focus of libidinal investment and masturbatory activity, although the child remains incapable of genital fulfilment with another person. The final 'genital' stage, in which the individual becomes capable of fully satisfying sexual relations with the opposite sex, is not reached until after puberty; and, even in the most maturely developed characters, traces of earlier stages of libidinal development can always be detected.

In Freud's original account of the infant's sexual development the emphasis is upon *auto-erotism*; that is, upon changes taking place in the infant's own body, rather than in its relationships. Freud thought that the infant was transiently attached to the mother's breast in the oral stage, but that the oral component instinct then detached itself and found satisfaction in such activities as thumb-sucking and chewing. Although Freud continued to be aware of trauma as a cause of disturbance, he pictured the infant's development as an internal process only tenuously connected with interaction with the mother or other care-takers. It was not until near the end of Freud's life that he began to appreciate the signal importance of the infant's relationship with the mother. Before this, mothers were considered chiefly as agents who answered the infant's needs by relieving accumulated tensions which the infant feared as dangerous. Mothers were not perceived as persons with whom the infant interacted emotionally and who provided stimulation and opportunities for learning as well as the relief of tension.

Freud pictured the infant's sexuality as 'polymorphously perverse': that is, as diffusely composed of component instincts which at first are separate tendencies, but which finally coalesce at a later stage to form the adult sexual drive. Amongst these component instincts are sadistic and masochistic impulses, homosexual interests, exhibitionistic and voyeuristic tendencies, and fetishistic preoccupations. Traces of all these components can be found in the normal person, but they are particularly emphasized in neurotics. Freud now suggested that neurotic symptoms were the consequence of the repression of *perverse* sexual impulses dating from the earliest years. Because of this early repression, the neurotic's sexuality remained partly undeveloped. When one or other component instinct had become exaggerated, but had not been repressed, the person concerned became a sexual pervert: that is, he acted out his perverse tendency in real life. Both neurotics and perverts, therefore, were fixated at early stages of sexual development, but dealt with this fixation differently. It was this observation which led to Freud's well-known statement that

> *neuroses are, so to say, the negative of perversions*
>
> *(SE, VII.165).*

At the end of the nineteenth century, many investigators were interested in the vagaries of human sexuality; but Freud was the most influential in persuading both doctors and the general public that sexual perversions are disorders of psycho-sexual development, not 'hereditary taints' or manifestations of 'degeneration'. He particularly emphasized the bisexuality of both men and women.

In some persons, traces of early stages of libidinal development were so persistent that it became customary to refer to 'oral' or to 'anal' characters. Oral traits of character were largely worked out by Freud's disciple, Karl Abraham. Freud himself, as one might expect from the character sketch given in the first chapter of this book, concentrated upon anal traits. No one paid much attention to describing phallic traits of character; but Rycroft, in his dictionary of psycho-analysis, refers to the phallic character as

> a person who conceives of sexual behaviour as a display of potency, in contrast to the genital character, who conceives of it as participation in a relationship.

Of a variety of oral characteristics described, passivity, dependency, and doubts about one's own competence are those most often linked. These traits are commonly found together in persons prone to recurrent depression. Some people exhibiting these features of personality are also given to 'oral' habits, like thumb-sucking, overeating, and over-indulgence in alcohol and tobacco; patterns of behaviour which have been considered by psycho-analysts as compensatory for an original sense of deprivation at the breast. In the case of sexual perverts, a particular preoccupation with *cunnilingus* and *fellatio*, or even with kissing, to the detriment of coitus, would be deemed evidence of persisting oral psychopathology. But the research evidence linking actual deprivation with the later development of oral behaviour or character is weak. It is best to regard orality as a useful piece of clinical observation without being specific about its cause.

The same holds good for the 'anal' character. Preoccupation with orderliness and cleanliness was considered to be a 'reaction-formation' against a particularly marked concern with the messiness and dirt associated with defecation. Obstinacy was interpreted as deriving from rebellion against parental insistence that excretion should take place only in particular circumstances. Parsimony was related to the infant's desire to obtain pleasure by holding on to its faeces for as long as possible; for, as Freud demonstrated from myths, fairy tales, and popular speech, money and faeces are often associated in phrases like 'filthy lucre', and 'tight-arsed'. In perverts, rather than neurotics, preoccupation with excretion and with the anal orifice is easily demonstrated as, for example, in de Sade's *Les 120 Journées de Sodome*.

Research designed to discover whether or not obsessional neurosis and 'anal' traits of character are the consequence of severe or eccentric methods of toilet-training has not found any consistent causal connection. But the traits which Freud described as being associated are in fact found together quite frequently. Although Freud's causal explanation receives little support, his clinical observation and descriptions are accurate.

The Oedipus complex

We come now to the vexed questions of the Oedipus complex, childhood amnesia, and the so-called latency period which is supposed to follow the Oedipal phase. Freud's formulation of the Oedipus complex originated from his self-analysis. In a letter to Fliess dated 15 October 1897, Freud wrote:

> My self-analysis is in fact the most essential thing I have at present and promises to become of the greatest value to me if it reaches its end. . . . It is by no means easy. Being totally honest with oneself is a good exercise. A single idea of general value dawned on me. I have found, in my own case too, [the phenomenon of] being in love with my mother and jealous of my father, and I now consider it a universal event in early childhood, even if not so early in children who have been made hysterical. (Similar to the invention of parentage

[family romance] in paranoia – heroes, founders of religion). If this is so, we can understand the gripping power of *Oedipus Rex*, in spite of all the objections that reason raises against the presupposition of fate; and we can understand why the later 'drama of fate' was bound to fail so miserably (*The Freud-Fliess Letters*, 271–2).

Freud came to assume that, by the time he has reached the 'phallic' stage of development, at around the age of 4 or 5, the small boy is sexually interested in his mother, wishes to gain exclusive possession of her, and therefore harbours hostile impulses towards his father. However, the hostility arouses fear that the father will retaliate, and the form which this retaliation is likely to take is that of castration. The 'castration complex' is activated partly by threats of castration from adults who have observed him masturbating, and partly by the little boy's assumption that, because girls are without a penis, they must have suffered castration. Confronted by what he perceives as a horrifying threat to the most precious part of his body, the small boy unconsciously abandons his hopes of sexual union with his mother, identifies himself with his potentially aggressive father, and finally turns his attention towards securing sexual satisfaction from other feminine sources.

The female version of the Oedipus complex is less clearly worked out, in line with the fact that Freud continued to find women a puzzle throughout his life. However, Freud concluded that, while the little girl is also at first involved emotionally with her mother, her discovery that she lacks a penis, and is therefore an inferior being, leads her to become disillusioned with her mother whom she blames for her condition. This turns her towards her father as a love object, and she begins to phantasize that he will impregnate her. The resulting child, Freud supposes, will compensate the girl for her lack of a penis, and, in this sense, might be said to be a substitute for the missing organ. What brings this stage of emotional development to a conclusion is the girl's growing perception of other men as potential impregnators who will enable her to have a baby and thus overcome her continuing sense of being an inferior kind of human being.

Stated in so bald a fashion, Freud's perception of the Oedipus complex as constituting the central emotional stage through which every human being has to pass if she or he is to achieve adult stability and happiness sounds crude indeed. We have already observed that Freud invariably strove to reduce the psychological and emotional to the physical. To allege that all small boys fear castration at the hands of their fathers sounds ridiculous when taken literally. But, if we were to phrase it differently, and affirm that small boys are greatly concerned with establishing their identity as male persons, feel rivalry with their fathers, and are easily made to feel humiliated or threatened by disparaging remarks about their size, weakness, incapacity, and lack of experience, most people would concur.

Moreover, both small boys and men do feel that their genitals are an especially vulnerable part of their anatomy. Freud's contention that castration anxiety is greater in men, whilst fear of loss of love is greater in women, is supported by research. Females fear penetration, but because their sexual organs are less exposed, are not so prone to fear actual injury. Male genitals are not only unprotected, but also exquisitely sensitive to pain, as the torturers of the world have long appreciated. Enquiry among children attending a paediatric clinic revealed that a substantial minority had supposed that girls originally possessed a penis, but had lost it in one way or another. Castration anxiety has become part of day-to-day speech. Those familiar with psycho-analytic jargon often use it as a kind of shorthand. Thus, a man might say, 'I feel castrated', if, for some reason, he was unable to drive his car or carry on with his work. Freud's persistent attempt to abolish the metaphorical in favour of the literal has contributed to a widespread misunderstanding of what he had to say.

The same comments apply to the notion of 'penis envy'. In Freud's era, male dominance was even more evident than it is today. Because men hold most of the power, many women consider themselves inferior, unappreciated, despised, or weak. Producing babies is one way in which women can feel equal or

25

superior to men. If we express Freud's idea in psychological, rather than anatomical, terms, very few people would take issue with it. As Jung is supposed to have remarked, 'After all, the penis is only a phallic symbol.'

In putting forward his ideas about infantile sexuality and the Oedipus complex, Freud was responsible for underlining the concept that the child is father to the man, emotionally and sexually, as well as in other ways. Freud was writing before zoologists had carried out the kind of experiments with subhuman primates which demonstrate that, for example, prolonged isolation in infancy renders the adult animal incapable of mating or forming normal social relationships. Today, we take it for granted that a child's intimate relationship with each parent, including physical closeness, is likely to affect its future capacity for making warm, affectionate relationships with its peers when it grows up; and the fact that we make such an assumption is largely due to Freud, even though we may not now agree with everything which he had to say about childhood.

Freud thought of the Oedipus complex as a universal; but it can be argued that it is very much a Western concept which particularly applies to the small, 'nuclear' family. Do children brought up in extended families, in which polygamy is the norm, experience the jealousy, possessiveness, and fear which Freud found in his patients? We do not know; but anecdotal evidence suggests the contrary. A Nigerian analyst told me that, during his training analysis, it took him over a year to make his analyst understand the entirely different emotional climate which obtains in a family in which the father has several wives.

We have already observed that Freud, at least in the early stages of his thought, was more concerned with the child's relation with the father than with its relation with the mother. Moreover, the father was also portrayed as authoritarian and severe; the source of prohibitions and threats; and the origin of what later became called the 'super-ego'. Modern research supports Freud's idea of a stage of male development in which the boy feels rivalry with the father; but indicates that the boy's subsequent identification with the father is not 'identification with the aggressor' but because the father makes friendly, loving overtures. As Fisher and Greenberg put it:

It would appear that he [the boy] gives up his acute competitive stance vis-à-vis father because father transmits friendly positive messages inviting him to join up rather than fight . . . He invites his son to draw close, to form an alliance, to adopt his identity, and to accept his values (p. 222).

Infantile amnesia

Most human beings can recall very little of their earliest childhood. Enquiry has demonstrated that 'first memories' date from about 3.2 years. Freud attributed infantile amnesia to repression, assuming that everyone would prefer to banish to the unconscious their earliest sexual impulses and experiences. This seems improbable, especially in cultures in which sexual play between children evokes amusement rather than horror. There are more likely reasons. Research shows that the growth of memory is a gradual process. Registration, retention, and recall are all less efficient before the development of language. No one knows how well children of, say, 3 or 4 recall events from still earlier periods, memory for which will disappear. But, even in adults, memory for recent events is transient unless it is refreshed by rehearsal. Without a capacity for language, rehearsal does not occur; and so it is not surprising that, before language is fairly well developed, memories are not well retained.

The latency period

Freud believed that the Oedipal phase was succeeded by a 'latency period', lasting from about 5 until puberty, in which sexual impulses and behaviour, though not abolished, were much less in evidence. Research does not support this latter supposition. In sexually permissive cultures, sex play is common throughout the years of middle childhood; and even in cultures in which sex play is frowned upon, and hence concealed, the evidence is that masturbation, heterosexual play, and homosexual play all increase with every year that passes.

27

However, Freud was right in his perception that human growth and development are diphasic. From birth to 5, the pace is rapid. Then comes a phase in which the growth curve rises less steeply, to be succeeded by another spurt just before puberty. Human adaptation largely depends upon learning and the transmission of culture. For these to take place effectively, the period of childhood dependency has to be prolonged, and it is probably for this reason that a phase of slower development, corresponding to the latency period, has been interposed between the two rapid phases. Many common human problems can justifiably be related to the prolongation of immaturity and dependence on parents. Freud's perception that the parent of the opposite sex constituted the child's first sexual object goes some way towards explaining a number of sexual difficulties experienced by adults. A man or woman who has not broken free of emotional ties with parents is likely to perceive potential sexual partners partly as if they were parents. This complicates the relationship, both sexually and in other ways. According to Freud, the Oedipal attachment to the parent of the opposite sex (at least in the male) is accompanied by the threat of castration. Men who continue to perceive women chiefly or partly as mothers may, therefore, regard them as potentially dangerous as well as sexually attractive; and this perception is likely to cause a variety of sexual difficulties, including turning away from women altogether, partial or complete impotence, or the need for reassuring devices like sadomasochistic rituals or fetishes before intercourse is possible. Various details of the Oedipal theory are open to question, but the general outline stands as powerfully explanatory of a variety of sexual difficulties and ways of behaving which had previously appeared inexplicable.

Where Freud was wrong was in making psychosexual development so central that all other forms of social and emotional development were conceived as being derived from it. In his essay on Leonardo, Freud even derives curiosity and the desire for knowledge from sexuality. He must have been aware that many animals exhibit exploratory behaviour which is obviously adaptive in providing information about the environment. Such behaviour seems more closely analogous to human intellectual curiosity; but Freud so insists upon sex as the prime mover that he regards sublimated *infantile sexual researches* as providing the motive power for a subsequent passion for knowledge. Today, most students of childhood development regard sexual development as only one link in the chain, not as a prime cause. Difficulties in interpersonal relationships may be derived from early insecurities which have nothing to do with sex, but which may cause later sexual problems. Similarly, difficulties in sexual development may cause subsequent social problems.

4 Free association, dreams, and transference

Free association

Pari passu with the development of his theory of neurosis, Freud was altering his technique of treatment. From 1892 onwards, he gradually abandoned hypnosis in favour of free association. The patient was still required to recline on a couch, with Freud sitting out of sight at its head; but attempts at urging the patient to recover memories by hypnosis or by using pressure on the forehead were given up. Instead, the patient was required to put into words without censorship whatever thoughts or phantasies spontaneously occurred to her. This change in technique had consequences which have had a lasting influence, not only upon psycho-analysis, but upon most subsequent forms of psychotherapy, and upon many other situations in which one human being is endeavouring to help another. The employment of free association compels the patient to take the initiative, and makes the psycho-analyst assume a much more passive attitude than that conventionally expected of a doctor. Hypnosis is a treatment which is principally dependent upon the patient's compliance and the doctor's authority. Free association requires the patient to retain a larger measure of autonomy. Thus, psycho-analysis became a technique of helping the patient to help him or herself. Instead of looking to the psycho-analyst for direct advice, positive suggestions, or specific instructions, the patient had to learn to use psycho-analysis as a means of understanding herself better. It was hoped that, armed with new insight, she would then be able to solve her own problems.

Dreams

If a patient lying on the couch engages in free association, she is likely, from time to time, to tell the psycho-analyst about her dreams, since dreams are often impressive or disturbing mental phenomena. Although there was an extensive literature on the subject of dreams before Freud turned his attention to it, Freud is justly famous for pulling the threads together, for making the dream into a legitimate object of scrutiny, and for creating a theory of dreams and a technique for interpreting them.

The Interpretation of Dreams was first published in November 1899. While staying at the Schloss Bellevue, outside Vienna, in July 1895, Freud had dreamed his famous dream of 'Irma's injection'. The details of this dream, which has provoked a vast literature, need not concern us. Freud's reading of the dream was that it was an attempt to absolve him from the responsibility of mishandling the treatment of a particular patient, and thus represented the fulfilment of a wish. In 1900, he was staying there again, and on 12 June wrote to Fliess:

> Do you suppose that someday one will read on a marble tablet on this house:
>
> > Here, on July 24, 1895,
> > the secret of the dream
> > revealed itself to Dr. Sigm. Freud
> >
> > (*The Freud-Fliess Letters*, 417)

Freud's phantasy became reality on 6 May 1977, when such a plaque was placed there.

In 1931 Freud wrote a preface to the third English edition of *The Interpretation of Dreams* in which he said:

> This book, with the new contribution to psychology which surprised the world when it was published (1900), remains essentially unaltered. It contains, even according to my present-day judgement, the most valuable of all the discoveries it has been my good fortune to make. Insight such as this falls to one's lot but once in a lifetime.
>
> (*SE*, IV.xxxii)

Creative innovators are not always the best judges of their own works. Freud's theory of dreams, although still influential, has not stood the test of time unmodified, as Freud believed it would. His final theory was incubating for a long period, for Freud had been interested in dreams when he was a medical student, years before the birth of psycho-analysis. We need not record the stages through which the theory passed; but simply state it in its final form.

Freud affirmed that, with very few exceptions, dreams were disguised, hallucinatory fulfilments of repressed wishes. He also asserted that dreams not only represented current wishes, but were also invariably expressions of wish-fulfilments dating from early childhood. This theory is clearly derived from, or comparable with, Freud's early statement about hysteria quoted in Chapter 2, in which he supposed that the trauma which provoked the current symptoms did so only because it awoke memories of traumata in childhood. Freud regarded dreams as if they were neurotic symptoms. Since normal people dream, Freud's theory of dreams supported the idea that neurotic and normal cannot be sharply distinguished, and paved the way for establishing psycho-analysis as a general theory of the mind which applied to everyone.

It also ingeniously reinforced his fundamental conviction that nearly all neurotic problems originated in early childhood. Dreams, he believed, gave indirect expression to infantile sexual wishes which had been repressed and which, if expressed in undisguised form, would so disturb the dreamer that he would wake up.

> Our theory of dreams regards wishes originating in infancy as the indispensable motive force for the formation of dreams.
> (*SE*, V.589)

Because these wishes are unacceptable and potentially disturbing, they are censored and disguised. The emergent dream, like a neurotic symptom, is a compromise between censorship and direct expression. The events of the previous day, which often enter into dreams, are important only because they resonate with, and therefore activate, the repressed infantile impulse.

Freud described the mental processes, or 'dream-work', by which the dream was modified and rendered less disturbing. These processes included condensation, the fusing together of different ideas and images into a single image; displacement, in which a potentially disturbing image or idea is replaced by something connected but less disturbing; representation, the process by which thoughts are converted into visual images; and symbolization, in which some neutral object stands for, or alludes to, some aspect of sexual life or those persons connected with it which the dreamer would prefer not to recognize. In addition, Freud referred to secondary revision; a process which strives to make the dream intelligible by converting it into a coherent story and, in doing so, probably distorts it still further.

This view implies that the dream as recalled by the dreamer had previously been subjected to a complex process of disguise which concealed its real meaning. Freud introduced the term 'manifest content' to describe what the dreamer recalled. In contrast, the 'latent content' was the hidden, true meaning of the dream, which could be ascertained only when the dreamer's associations to the images in the dream had been subjected to psycho-analytical scrutiny and interpretation.

Freud's dream theory reflects both his single-mindedness and his tendency to generalization. He was sure that he was right in asserting that infantile sexual wishes were the root cause of neurosis. Dreams, in Freud's view, were primitive, irrational mental phenomena which ignored logic, syntax, and the consciously accepted criteria defining time and space. But ´

The interpretation of dreams is the royal road to a knowledge of the unconscious activities of the mind (SE, V.608).

Dreams, therefore, must needs be primarily concerned with infantile sexuality, the single 'indispensable organic foundation' of psycho-analytic theory, even if, at first sight, many of them appeared to be concerned with quite other matters.

Freud's technique of dream interpretation is notably ingenious; but even he had to admit that certain types of dream did not fit his theory. First, there are dreams which do not require interpretation. A hungry person dreams of food; a thirsty person dreams of drinking. These so-called 'convenience' dreams certainly express wishes, but refer only to the present state of the dreamer and not to his infancy.

Secondly, there are 'traumatic' dreams which repeat, in undisguised form, some unexpected, shocking event like a car accident, a bomb incident, or an unprovoked attack like rape or other physical assault. Freud eventually admitted that such dreams could not be regarded as fulfilling wishes. He believed that they occurred when the trauma had been so sudden that the mind of the individual had had no opportunity to shield itself against shock by anxious preparation. He wrote:

> These dreams are endeavouring to master the stimulus retrospectively, by developing the anxiety whose omission was the cause of the traumatic neurosis (*SE*, XVIII.32).

Freud, although concerned with the 'compulsion to repeat' in this paper, does not mention the fact that individuals who have been exposed to trauma consciously behave in the same way as their dreams indicate: that is, they strive to come to terms with, or master, their shock by repeatedly telling the story of their trauma to anyone who will listen. 'Bomb stories' following air raids in the Second World War often became tedious.

Thirdly, anxiety dreams, sometimes amounting to nightmares, appear to contradict Freud's theory of wish-fulfilment. Freud explained such dreams in two ways. First, it might be that anxiety pertained to the manifest content only. Analysis would surely demonstrate that the latent content contained a wish-fulfilment. Or it might be that repression and the dreamwork had partially failed, thus allowing some of the anxiety connected with forbidden impulses to manifest itself. In this case, the dreamer usually awoke, for such dreams also fail to fulfil their function as guardians of sleep. It should be added that, at the time when Freud formulated his theory of dreams, he thought that anxiety was simply a manifestation of undischarged sexual energy. Later, in his book *Inhibitions, Symptoms and Anxiety*, he came to regard anxiety as a signal pointing to a possible danger threatening the ego, which made the individual feel helpless. For example, a child might feel incapable of discharging, or otherwise coping with, aggressive or sexual impulses arising from within. Or he might feel threatened from without by the loss of a parent who provided both love and protection. Freud did not modify his dream theory to include this new interpretation of anxiety.

Fourthly, both men and women not infrequently have sexual dreams which culminate in orgasm. The imagery in such dreams may either be symbolic or else undisguised. Freudians have attempted to explain this by alleging that the sexual wishes which appear overtly are those which are acceptable to the dreamer, whilst those which appear in symbolic form are unacceptable; but this does not explain dreams in which sexual impulses are both openly expressed and also distressing to the dreamer. The idea that dreams invariably conceal repressed wishes is not tenable.

Although Freud tenaciously maintained that repressed infantile wishes were the main instigators of dreams, most of the clinical examples which he furnishes are concerned with the emotions of adult life: with rivalry, inappropriate sexual desires, or, as in the case of his own dream about Irma, with the wish to be absolved from blame. Today, very few psycho-analysts support Freud's theory in its original form. Although some dreams are certainly concerned with unfulfilled or disreputable wishes, this is not true of all dreams. Moreover, if dreams were all expressions of repressed infantile impulses which found an indirect way past the censor, one would expect that the proportion of sleep spent in dreaming would increase with age. In reality, electroencephalographic studies show that infants spend more time dreaming than do adults; information which was not available to Freud. Dreams are not couched in the language of everyday speech, but it does not follow that they are necessarily concealing something unacceptable. Poetry is a kind of human utterance in which symbol and metaphor play a predominant role. Poetry may often be hard to

35

understand, but we do not usually think of it as wilfully obscure on this account.

A symbol may be defined as 'whatever stands for something, or has representative function'. A banal example is a national flag. 'Freudian symbols' are popularly supposed to be objects occurring in dreams or phantasies which represent the genitals. Thus, hollow containers, like caves or handbags, may symbolize the female genitals; while swords, umbrellas, or pencils may be taken as indicating the penis. As Rycroft has pointed out in his essay, 'Is Freudian Symbolism a Myth?', Freud did not at first attach great significance to sexual symbolism, and only came to do so because of the work of Wilhelm Stekel. Having recognized the importance of symbolization, Freud treated it in typically reductive fashion. That is, he stated that:

> The very great majority of symbols in dreams are sexual symbols (*SE*, XV. 153).

and goes on to list a large number of objects of the kind referred to above. In other words, symbols are treated by Freud as predominantly serving the function of concealment, or of making the anatomical aspects of sexuality more acceptable. As we shall see in Chapter 8, which is concerned with Freud's views on art and literature, Freud took a similarly negative view of phantasy, which he regarded as primarily escapist.

If, unlike Freud, we regard the development of an inner world of the imagination and the development of the capacity for symbolization as adaptive functions which march hand in hand and which are especially highly developed in man, it is possible to see that symbols can have the positive function of bridging the gap between the inner world and the external world and of giving objects in the external world emotional significance. The 'transitional objects' described by Winnicott in his paper of 1951 in *Through Paediatrics to Psychoanalysis* (1975) are typical examples. Very young children develop powerful attachments to inanimate objects from which they are reluctant to be parted, like teddy bears or bits of blanket. Such objects originally symbolize the mother. But, since these symbolic objects actually exist, they cannot be dismissed as merely imaginary. Nor can the process of symbolization which gives these objects significance be regarded as escapist, since a transitional object acts as a real comforter. As we shall see in subsequent chapters, Freud's rigid division of mental activities into rational and irrational, or 'secondary process', and 'primary process', causes endless difficulties.

Freud's theory of dreams seems to be based upon the supposition that, because repression is the mechanism for banishing what is unacceptable to the unconscious, everything unconscious carries a negative sign. In a paper on 'The Unconscious', written in 1915, Freud states that 'the repressed does not cover everything that is unconscious' (*SE*, XIV.166); but there is little sign of this in his original dream theory. There are many reasons for thinking that what is unconscious is not exclusively, or even predominantly, the consequence of repression, including the fact that some dreams are clearly creative or provide answers to problems. Modern theorists are inclined to think of dreams in terms of information processing; perhaps something to do with comparing the experiences of the day with similar experiences which are stored in the long-term memory. But, in spite of the deficiencies in Freud's theory of dreams, it is important to recognize that it was Freud who reinstated the dream as a phenomenon deserving study.

Transference

The other notable consequence which followed Freud's adoption of free association was his discovery of transference. Transference was originally defined as the process by which a patient attributes to his analyst attitudes and ideas that derive from previous figures in his life, especially from his parents. The term has now been extended to include the patient's total emotional attitude towards the analyst. If a patient is encouraged to say everything which comes into her mind without censorship, she will talk not only about her neurotic symptoms and early childhood memories, but about her hopes and fears, her successes and failures, and also about her current relationships, including her relationship, or lack of relationship, with the psycho-analyst.

As a scientist and medical man, Freud's original hope was that he had discovered both the cause of neurotic symptoms and also a treatment which would abolish them. By enabling the patient to circumvent repression and recall the vicissitudes of her infantile development, the blocks which were preventing the proper discharge of instinctual impulses would be overcome, and the symptoms, which were the result of a compromise between repression and discharge, would disappear. According to this view, the treatment of neurosis was comparable with the treatment of physical illness. Just as tubercle bacilli might be regarded as the cause of pulmonary tuberculosis, and abolished by a strict regime of treatment, so neuroses were caused by repressed infantile impulses, and abolished by recall and abreaction of those impulses, thus overcoming the blocks which had obstructed the patient's progress towards sexual maturity. Psycho-analysis could therefore be regarded as a technique which could be learned like the technique of any other medical treatment; and the psychoanalyst could assume the traditional role of a skilled medical practitioner: benevolent, considerate, but essentially detached.

This is certainly the model which Freud originally attempted to follow; one in which the relationship between patient and doctor was professional and objective rather than personal, although personal elements like gratitude might be in evidence to a limited extent. Freud himself compared his role to that of a mountain guide. As we saw in Chapter 1, Freud was a particularly detached individual, regarded by at least one analysand as 'curiously impersonal'. When Freud abandoned hypnosis or using pressure on the forehead in favour of free association, it was no longer strictly necessary to enjoin patients to lie supine upon a couch. But Freud kept the couch and his own position out of sight of the patient, partly in order to facilitate the flow of the patient's associations, but partly, as he admitted, because he did not like being stared at for so many hours a day. His insistence upon his own anonymity and his refusal to answer questions about himself may also have had personal origins. We noted in Chapter 1 that Freud was extremely reluctant to reveal anything about himself. However, this reluctance proved in the end to be a powerful means of evoking phantasies from patients which would never have appeared if Freud had been more forthcoming. It is still an important aspect of contemporary techniques of psycho-therapy. It was Freud's detachment and refusal to become personally involved with his patients that both promoted the phenomena of transference and made those phenomena apparent.

When Freud found that he became emotionally important to his patients, his initial response was negative, although he quickly recognized that transference was a vital and unavoidable part of the psycho-analytic process. Freud at first thought of transference as an erotic attachment to the psycho-analyst, as indeed it can be. However deplorable this might be, it was, so Freud believed, a useful way of overcoming the resistances of the patient. Later, Freud came to think of transference as an artificially induced neurosis in which the patient repeated all the attitudes which she had held towards her parents. By means of interpretation, Freud strove to convert this repetition into recollection, thus reducing the intensity of the patient's present emotions by affirming that they really belonged to the past.

As late as 5 June 1910, Freud was still exhibiting distaste for transference, in spite of recognizing its importance. In a letter to Pfister, he wrote:

As for the transference, it is altogether a curse. The intract-able and fierce impulses in the illness, on account of which I renounced both indirect and hypnotic suggestion, cannot be altogether abolished even through psycho-analysis; they can only be restrained, and what remains expresses itself in the transference. That is often a considerable amount.

One can understand Freud's feelings. He had hoped that his patients would accept him simply as a skilled physician who could, by means of his technique, expose the origins and abolish the symptoms of their neuroses. Instead, they made him into an idealized lover, a father-figure, or a saviour. What they wanted was not his science, but his love.

It is surely because Freud was by nature an impersonal investigator that he interpreted his patients' emotional impulses towards him as being entirely repetitions from the past, and discounted the possibility that they might be experiencing genuine feelings in the here-and-now.

> The patient, that is to say, directs toward the physician a degree of affectionate feeling (mingled, often enough, with hostility) which is based on no real relationship between them and which—as is shown by every detail of its emergence—can only be traced back to old wishful phantasies of the patient's which have become unconscious.
> (*SE*, XI.51)

In fact, it is perfectly natural that patients should genuinely value the psycho-analyst, however much their picture of him or her may be distorted by past experience. Many patients seeking psycho-analysis have never experienced from anyone else the kind of long-term concern which is offered in psycho-analysis. There is no other situation in life in which one can count on a devoted listener for so many hours. What many patients experience is an awakening of emotions which they have never had, rather than a repetition of phantasies from the past. The majority of contemporary psycho-analysts believe that neurosis is not so much a matter of inhibited or underdeveloped sexuality as of a wider failure to make satisfying human relationships on equal terms. Interpretation of transference, therefore, depends upon the psycho-analyst detecting and commenting upon the way in which the patient is relating to him in the present: whether he is fearful, compliant, aggressive, competitive, and so on. Such attitudes have their history, which needs to be explored; but the emphasis is on understanding in what way the patient's attitude to others is distorted through perceiving in what way his attitude to the analyst is distorted. To do this effectively requires that the psycho-analyst is not concerned solely with the events of early childhood, but also recognizes that there is a real relationship in the here-and-now.

It soon became obvious to Freud that the psycho-analyst was not, and could not be, the kind of detached observer who was no more affected by his patient than if the latter was a chemical solution. In 1910 Freud wrote:

> Other innovations in technique relate to the physician himself. We have become aware of the 'counter-transference', which arises in him as a result of the patient's influence on his unconscious feelings, and we are almost inclined to insist that he shall recognize the counter-transference in himself and overcome it (*SE*, XI.144–5).

Freud originally hoped that this could be accomplished by a self-analysis comparable with his own. He later recognized that self-analysis should be replaced by a training analysis conducted by another person. In fact, Jung was the first of the early psycho-analysts to insist that the analyst must himself be analysed. The psycho-analyst must monitor his own emotional responses by means of introspection, since his own, subjective response to the patient's discourse is an inescapable part of understanding him.

This is a far cry from the mental set demanded of a scientist, who must on no account allow his emotions to affect any experiment which he is conducting. Although the psycho-analyst must, to some extent, regard his patient objectively, he will only be able to understand the patient as a person if he is also able to use his own, subjective reactions. The total detachment which Freud aimed at, but which, as we know from contemporary accounts of his behaviour as an analyst, he never achieved, would have cut him off from sources of information that we all need if we are to comprehend persons as opposed to comprehending the external world. In spite of his recognition of transference and counter-transference, Freud continued to maintain that he was a scientist until his death. His psycho-analytic endeavours might be more justly compared with those of a historian. Historians also try to reconstruct the past, but no one supposes that a totally objective vision of the past can ever be achieved, or that a history which attempted this would be anything but unreadable. A historian's understanding of the past and of the motives of the people who make history is bound to be influenced by his own experience and by his capacity for understanding human beings. This is why neither history nor psycho-analysis can be assigned to the exact sciences.

5 Ego, super-ego, and id

Although Freud generally resisted modifications of his ideas when suggested by others, he constantly revised them himself, and retained his capacity for creative innovation until the end of his long life. During the latter part of the First World War and the early 1920s, Freud made extensive additions to, and revisions of psycho-analytic theory. The most important of these concern narcissism, the structure of the mental apparatus, and recognition of the significance of aggressive impulses in addition to sexual ones.

Narcissism

This is a term originally used to describe a sexual perversion in which the subject is in love with himself rather than with another person. It was later extended to include any form of self-love. Since self-esteem is necessary to psychic health, some degree of narcissism is considered normal. Freud thought that everyone directed libido both toward the self (ego-libido), and towards others (object-libido). When a person is in love, the greater part of his libido is invested in his beloved. When a person is ill, either physically or mentally, he becomes more self-absorbed, and less capable of emotional involvement with others. Extreme forms of narcissism are exhibited in the type of schizophrenia in which everything that happens in the world is interpreted by the sufferer as referring to himself; in manic states in which the subject considers himself omnipotent; and in states of depression in which the subject may be hypochondriacally preoccupied with his own state of body and mind to the exclusion of all else. Freud postulated a narcissistic stage of emotional development, or primary narcissism, which precedes any investment of libido in objects other than the self. He described this stage as one in which the sexual instincts find auto-erotic satisfaction. Mental or physical illness, therefore, may be considered as instituting regression to an early stage of infantile development.

Hitherto, Freud had assumed two sets of instincts: the self-preservative instincts, which pertained to the ego; and the sexual instincts, which pertained to objects. Now he concluded that self-preservation and self-love were really the same thing, and that what mattered was the degree to which libido was directed towards objects as compared with the degree to which it was directed towards the self.

As Ernest Jones commented in the second volume of his biography of Freud, Freud's paper 'On Narcissism: An Introduction' (*SE*, XIV.73–102) played into the hands of those critics who accused Freud of reducing everything to sex. Originally, Freud had assumed that the self-preservative instincts were distinct from the sexual instincts, and could be in conflict with them. By affirming that love of others was self-love turned outward, Freud appeared to be stating that sexual impulses were indeed the sole source of psychic energy. This position was soon to be modified.

Freud was essentially a dualist who habitually explained mental phenomena in terms of the interaction of, or conflict between, opposites. As he would have been the first to recognize, the tendency to think in this way is characteristic of obsessional personalities, who are notably 'ambivalent' towards the people with whom they are involved, and who often have difficulty in making decisions because they cannot reconcile opposing considerations. Love and hate are opposites which can be clearly discerned in any intense relationship between people; and when such a relationship is ruptured, love often appears to be transmuted into hatred. Freud came to the conclusion that hate was closely connected with the ego's struggle for self-preservation. He went on to state that:

Hate, as a relation to objects, is older than love. It derives from the narcissistic ego's primordial repudiation of the external world with its outpouring of stimuli. As an expression of the reaction of unpleasure evoked by objects, it always remains in an intimate relation with the self-preservative instincts; so that sexual and ego-instincts can readily develop an antithesis which repeats that of love and hate (*SE*, XIV.139).

The reference to 'the external world with its outpouring of stimuli' may appear obscure unless it is recalled that one of Freud's fundamental ideas was that the organism is always seeking to rid itself of disturbing stimuli, whether these impinge upon it from the external world, or originate as instinctual tensions from within. In Chapter 2 reference was made to 'the need of the organism to reach a state of tranquillity by completely discharging all tensions'. Freud continued to maintain that:

> the nervous system is an apparatus which has the function of getting rid of the stimuli which reach it, or of reducing them to the lowest possible level; or which, if it were feasible, would maintain itself in an altogether unstimulated condition (*SE*, XIV.120).

Freud's original studies of hysteria and obsessional neurosis required a bipartite division of mind into conscious and unconscious. This simple model assumed that the unconscious was chiefly, if not entirely, derived from repression, and therefore consisted of impulses, thoughts and feelings which were unacceptable to the conscious ego. During the first twenty years of the twentieth century, Freud came to realize that this model was inadequate. For example, the agency instituting repression must be derived from the ego, the conscious part of the mind. Yet, patients on the couch behaved as if this agency was unconscious by manifesting *resistance*. That is, when dangerous or distasteful topics began to emerge during free association, the patient would cease to talk freely, claim that no thoughts occurred to him, say that he had forgotten what was being discussed, or in other ways become evasive. Freud said that the

> force which instituted the repression and maintains it is perceived as *resistance* during the work of analysis (*SE*, XIX.14).

But this implied that part of the ego, hitherto associated only with consciousness, could itself be unconscious. Freud recognized that the term 'unconscious' was better used as a descriptive adjective rather than as a topographical noun. Although everything which was repressed was unconscious, not everything unconscious was repressed.

Structure of the mental apparatus

Freud's new model of the mind which was the consequence of these and other reflections consisted of three parts: ego, id, and super-ego. The id is defined as the oldest part of the mind from which the other structures are derived.

> It contains everything that is inherited, that is present at birth, that is laid down in the constitution – above all, therefore, the instincts which originate from the somatic organization and which find a first psychical expression here in forms unknown to us (*SE*, XXIII.145).

The id is primitive, unorganized, and emotional: 'the realm of the illogical'.

> It is the dark, inaccessible part of our personality; what little we know of it we have learnt from our study of the dream-work and of the construction of neurotic symptoms, and most of that is of a negative character and can be described only as a contrast to the ego. We approach the id with analogies: we call it a chaos, a cauldron full of seething excitations . . . It is filled with energy reaching it from the instincts, but it has no organization, produces no collective will, but only a striving to bring about the satisfaction of instinctive needs subject to the observance of the pleasure principle (*SE*, XXII.73).

Freud made a sharp distinction between two varieties of mental functioning which he called *primary process* and *secondary process*. The id uses primary process, which employs the mechanisms of condensation, displacement, symbolization, and hallucinatory wish-fulfilment to which we referred in Chapter 4 when discussing dreams. It also ignores the categories of time and space, and treats contraries like dark/light or high/deep as if they were identical. As indicated in Freud's description, the id is governed only by the most basic, primitive principle of mental dynamics: avoidance of 'unpleasure' caused by instinctual tension, which can only be achieved by satisfaction of instinctual needs accompanied by pleasure.

It is characteristic of Freud's predominantly pessimistic view of human nature that the so-called 'pleasure principle', upon which so much of his thought depends, is much more concerned with the avoidance of pain than with the pursuit of pleasure. In Chapter 2, we noted that powerful emotions were treated by Freud as disturbances which must be got rid of, not as pleasures to be sought.

The ego is that part of the mind representing consciousness. It employs secondary process: that is, reason, common sense, and the power to delay immediate responses to external stimuli or to internal instinctive promptings. It is originally derived from the id. Freud pictured the ego as a 'special organization' which is closely connected with the organs of perception, since it first develops as a result of stimuli from the external world impinging upon the senses.

'The ego is first and foremost a bodily ego' (*SE*, XIX.26).

Freud means by this that the ego, being originally derived from sensations springing from the surface of the body, is a projection of the surface of the body. The sense of 'I' depends upon the perception of one's own body as a separate entity. Once in existence, the ego 'acts as an intermediary between the id and the external world'. Because of the neural link between sensory perception and motor activity, the ego controls voluntary movement. The prime function of the ego is self-preservation.

As regards *external* events, it performs that task by becoming aware of stimuli, by storing up experiences about them (in the memory), by avoiding excessively strong stimuli (through flight), by dealing with moderate stimuli (through adaptation) and finally by bringing about expedient changes in the external world to its own advantage (through activity). As regards *internal* events, in relation to the id, it performs that task by gaining control over the demands of the instincts, by deciding whether they are to be allowed satisfaction, by postponing that satisfaction to times and circumstances favourable to the external world or by suppressing their excitations entirely (*SE*, XXIII.145–6).

Freud's third division of mind is described by him as follows:

The long period of childhood, during which the growing human being lives in dependence on his parents, leaves behind it as a precipitate the formation in his ego of a special agency in which this parental influence is prolonged. It has received the name of *super-ego*. In so far as this super-ego is differentiated from the ego or is opposed to it, it constitutes a third power which the ego must take into account.

(*SE*, XXIII.146)

The origin of Freud's concept of the super-ego can be traced to the paper on narcissism to which we referred earlier. Freud thought that, as the child developed, his megalomanic primary narcissism was gradually eclipsed: that is, he came no longer to regard himself as the omnipotent 'King Baby', as centre of the universe. As the child gradually acquires cultural and ethical ideas, his libidinal instinctual impulses undergo repression. Because of this split within the psyche, the child comes to realize that he can no longer idealize himself; that there is an *ego-ideal* to which his own ego does not always conform. Freud postulated an agency within the mind which devoted itself to *self-observation*: which watched the ego, and decided whether or not the ego was conforming to, or fell short of, the ego-ideal. This agency was what Freud later named the super-ego. As indicated in the last quotation, the super-ego originally derived from parental prohibitions and criticism. Because of the long period of childhood dependency, parental standards and subsequently the standards of society become introjected; that is, incorporated as part of the subject's own psyche with the consequence that the voice of conscience is heard whenever the ego falls short of the ego-ideal.

Freud might equally well have used Pavlovian terminology. The super-ego can be regarded as the product of repeated conditioning by parental injunctions and criticism: for example, 'You must clean your teeth after breakfast', may become so ingrained a command that the adult who has long ago left home continues to feel uncomfortable if he does not obey it.

The ego, therefore, is uneasily poised between three agencies: the external world, the id, and the super-ego, each of which may be urging a different course. It is not surprising that human actions sometimes appear vacillating or indecisive.

Aggression

Earlier in this chapter, we quoted Freud's conclusion that 'Hate, as a relation to objects, is older than love.' This sentence comes from a paper on 'Instincts and their Vicissitudes', written in 1915. It is Freud's first recognition of an 'aggressive instinct' as a constituent of the ego distinct from the sexual instinct. Before this period, Freud had regarded aggression as constituting a sadistic aspect of the sexual instinct; as 'an urge for mastery', a primitive form of striving for, and dominating, the sexual object.

Love in this form and at this preliminary stage is hardly to be distinguished from hate in its attitude toward the object. Not until the genital organization is established does love become the opposite of hate (*SE*, XIV.139).

Very slowly, in a roundabout fashion, Freud came to accept that there was an 'aggressive instinct' which was entirely independent of anything sexual.

I remember my own defensive attitude when the idea of an instinct of destruction first emerged in psycho-analytic

49

literature, and how long it took before I became receptive to it (*SE*, XXI.120).

Freud's frequent use of the word 'instinct' has an old-fashioned ring about it because modern psychologists and students of animal behaviour have largely abandoned the term. Instinct was originally used to describe aspects of behaviour which were thought to be innate and to develop independently of environmental influences. Today it is generally believed that all behaviour is influenced both by genetic constitution and by environmental conditions existing during development. Even relatively stereotyped forms of behaviour like bird-song may not manifest themselves unless the right environmental stimuli appear at the appropriate stage. There is a sense in which Freud was ahead of his time in postulating that the environment played such a large part in influencing sexual behaviour patterns. But there is no obvious reason other than his own preference for limiting 'instincts' to two. For example, sleep and eating are both largely determined by innate needs.

Freud's first full acknowledgement of an aggressive instinct appears in 'Beyond the Pleasure Principle', a speculative paper first published in 1920 (*SE*, XVIII.7–64). Although Freud continued to maintain that man was chiefly governed by the pleasure principle, modified, but not abolished, by the ego's acceptance of the reality principle, he concluded that another principle must also be in operation. As we saw in the last chapter, study of patients suffering from 'traumatic neurosis', that is, neuroses brought about by sudden accidents or shocks, revealed that their dreams often repeated the incident practically unmodified. Since the traumatic incident was, by definition, unpleasant, its repetition appeared to contravene the pleasure principle. Freud also noted that small children tended to repeat unpleasant experiences, like the departure of a parent, by making such happenings into a repetitive game which, in phantasy, gave them some control over the event. Freud concluded that both neurotics who had been exposed to shock and children who had been exposed to distress were attempting to master their unpleasant experiences by repeating them in dream and play.

At an earlier point in this chapter, we quoted Freud's view that hate was older than love, and connected with the ego's primordial rejection of objects as the origin of disturbing stimuli. Recalling this makes it comprehensible that Freud should link aggression with the mastery of shock and distress referred to above, and also with the tendency compulsively to repeat unpleasant experiences.

> The manifestations of a compulsion to repeat . . . exhibit to a high degree an instinctual character and, when they act in opposition to the pleasure principle, give the appearance of some 'daemonic' force at work (*SE*, XVIII.35).

But Freud goes further. Remaining true to his conception that the function of the mental apparatus is to get rid of the stimuli which reach it, he concludes that this daemonic, instinctual compulsion to repeat is a universal attribute of instincts. He writes:

> *It seems, then, that an instinct is an urge inherent in organic life to restore an earlier stage of things* which the living entity has been obliged to abandon under the pressure of external disturbing forces . . . (*SE*, XVIII.36).

And what is the earliest state of things which instinct is striving to restore? Since the inorganic precedes the organic in the history of our planet, it can only be a striving towards a state before life itself existed.

> If we are to take it as a truth that knows no exception that everything living dies for *internal* reasons – becomes inorganic once again – then we shall be compelled to say that '*the aim of all life is death*' and, looking backwards, that '*inanimate things existed before living ones*' (*SE*, XVIII.38).

The death instinct

This is Freud's assertion of what he now calls the 'death

instinct': the ultimate expression of the Nirvana principle, of the organism's striving to reach Swinburne's 'The Garden of Proserpine', where no stimuli from either within or without disturb its everlasting peace.

> Then star nor sun shall waken,
> Nor any change of light:
> Nor sound of waters shaken,
> Nor any sound or sight:
> Nor wintry leaves nor vernal,
> Nor days nor things diurnal;
> Only the sleep eternal
> In an eternal night.

These highly abstract considerations gave Freud what he wanted: a dualistic scheme in which all the phenomena of mental life could be ultimately traced to the interaction of, or conflict between, two drives or instincts.

> After long hesitancies and vacillations we have decided to assume the existence of only two basic instincts, *Eros* and *the destructive instinct*. . . . The aim of the first of these basic instincts is to establish ever greater unities and to preserve them thus – in short, to bind together; the aim of the second is, on the contrary, to undo connections and so to destroy things. In the case of the destructive instinct we may suppose that its final aim is to lead what is living into an inorganic state. For this reason we also call it the *death instinct*.
> (*SE*, XXIII.148)

Freud considered that aggression was derived from the death instinct being redirected towards the external world. He wrote:

> The instinct of destruction, moderated and tamed, and, as it were, inhibited in its aim, must, when it is directed toward objects, provide the ego with the satisfaction of its vital needs and with control over nature (*SE*, XXI.121).

Freud goes on to conclude that the inclination towards aggression 'constitutes the greatest impediment to civilization'. He pictures civilization as a process in the service of Eros, whose purpose is to combine single human individuals, and after that families, then races, peoples and nations, into one great unity, the unity of mankind. But man's natural aggressive instinct, the hostility of each against all and all against each, oppose this programme of civilization. This aggressive instinct is the derivative and the main representative of the death instinct which we have found alongside of Eros and which shares world-dominion with it. And now, I think, the meaning of the evolution of civilization is no longer obscure to us. It must present the struggle between Eros and Death, between the instinct of life and the instinct of destruction as it works itself out in the human species. This struggle is what all life essentially consists of, and the evolution of civilization may therefore be simply described as the struggle for life of the human species. And it is this battle of the giants that our nurse-maids try to appease with their lullaby about Heaven (*SE*, XXI.122).

Who would have supposed that a doctor striving to comprehend the neuroses of the Viennese upper classes would have derived from his researches so majestic a concept of the human condition? Freud's pursuit of the byways of sex and aggression has become transmuted into a cosmic vision of opposing forces of good and evil. Freud wrote the passage just quoted some seventeen years after his parting with Jung. If the two pioneers had continued to collaborate, Freud might have recognized that his portrayal of Eros and Death as giants locked in perpetual combat is what Jung would have called an 'archetypal' vision. Whether or not such a vision is true is another matter. It has nothing to do with science.

6 Aggression, depression, and paranoia

Having determined the existence of an independent 'destructive instinct', Freud addressed the problem of how civilization imposed controls upon it. He concluded that the main way in which this took place was by 'introjection'; that is, by incorporating a substantial amount of aggression within the ego of the individual, thus turning aggression away from the external world against the self. Freud is thus postulating a double redirection of aggression. The death instinct is originally directed against the self and, because every individual dies in the end, is ultimately triumphant. But, during the individual's lifetime, the death instinct is to a large extent directed outward as aggression: first, against unwanted stimuli from the external world; second, as 'sadism' subserving the domination of sexual objects; and third, against individuals or circumstances which frustrate the desires of the ego. However, civilization ensures that part of this destructiveness is again turned inward; incorporated into the super-ego, and manifested as the sense of guilt giving rise to self-reproach, self-hatred, and self-punishment.

> Civilization, therefore, obtains mastery over the individual's dangerous desire for aggression by weakening and disarming it and by setting up an agency within him to watch over it, like a garrison in a conquered city (*SE*, XXI.123–4).

Freud makes much of the irrational severity of the super-ego. He claims, with good reason, that a child who has been very leniently brought up may nevertheless develop a very strict conscience. His explanation of this is convincing. Freud believed that

> every piece of aggression whose satisfaction the subject gives up is taken over by the super-ego and increases the latter's aggressiveness (against the ego) (*SE*, XXI.129).

In other words, the more anyone inhibits his aggression towards others, the more likely he is to be self-punitive. Freud had previously described a similar state of affairs in a famous paper, 'Mourning and Melancholia'.

Melancholia would today be described as a severe depressive illness. Freud accurately describes its distinguishing mental features as

> a profoundly painful dejection, cessation of interest in the outside world, loss of the capacity to love, inhibition of all activity, and a lowering of the self-regarding feelings to a degree that finds utterance in self-reproaches and self-revilings, and culminates in a delusional expectation of punishment (*SE*, XIV.244).

In mourning, loss of self-regard is not usually present to the same extent, although many who have lost someone close to them do blame themselves for their own failure to love and care for the departed. In other respects, the mental features of mourning and severe depression are closely similar. Freud notes that mourning is often a very prolonged process, and attributes this difficulty in withdrawing libido from the departed love object to the more general difficulty which everyone has in abandoning any libidinal position: for example, the difficulty which neurotics have in abandoning Oedipal ties to parents.

Freud points out that melancholia is also often provoked by the loss of a loved person, although the loss may be provoked by rejection or abandonment rather than by death. But why should the depressed person heap reproaches on himself? Freud points out that the accusations which the person suffering from depression levels at himself are generally reproaches which he might equally have directed against the loved object who is no longer available. 'I am a worthless person who does not deserve to live' is a displacement of '*You* are a worthless person who does not deserve to live, because you have left me.' This is an example of one way in which aggression which was originally directed outward becomes displaced inward, incorporated into the super-ego; and then manifests itself as self-reproach and self-hatred.

According to Freud, the difference between mourning and melancholia primarily consists in the fact that, in mourning, the loss is fully conscious, whereas in melancholia, the loss is partially unconscious. How is this related to the difference between mourning and melancholia which we have already noted: the much greater loss of self-esteem in the latter condition? Freud accepts that, in a certain sense, the melancholic is telling the truth about his loss of self-esteem.

> The analogy with mourning led us to conclude that he had suffered a loss in regard to an object; what he tells us points to a loss in regard to his ego (*SE*, XIV.247).

What Freud suggests is illuminating. People who react to loss of an object by loss of self-esteem are people who base their choice of objects on identification with the object, that is, upon a narcissistic choice of an object which in some way resembles themselves. Losing an object, therefore, is equivalent to losing part of the ego. In the important paper, 'On Narcissism', to which reference was made in the last chapter, Freud listed a variety of ways in which objects are chosen.

A person may love:—

1) According to the narcissistic type:
   a) what he himself is (i.e. himself),
   b) what he himself was,
   c) what he himself would like to be,
   d) someone who was once part of himself.

2) According to the anaclitic (attachment) type:
   a) the woman who feeds him,
   b) the man who protects him,
      and the succession of substitutes who take their place (*SE*, XIV.90)

('Anaclitic' literally means 'leaning-on'. Freud is thinking of the original situation between the child and its mother: two objects, each of which receive some of the child's libidinal investment.) Freud is suggesting that melancholics are either regressing to, or have never fully emerged from, a primitive stage of emotional development in which their object-choices are narcissistic rather than anaclitic. Thus, when they lose an object, they are losing a greater part of themselves than are those whose love is more determined by attachment to an object who is quite different from themselves.

Freud thought of such patients as being arrested in the 'oral' stage of emotional development (see Chapter 3). The reasons for this arrest are not clearly specified; but it was assumed that fixation at the oral stage might be the result of either deprivation or overgratification of the infant's oral needs. Freud's single-minded explanation of the depressive personality in terms of arrest at the 'oral' stage of emotional development may be seen as insufficient in the light of modern research, but does not detract from the accuracy and penetration of his clinical description. We noted in Chapter 3 that passivity, dependency and doubts about one's own competence are traits of character often found together.

Today, we might describe the person prone to melancholia rather differently. The person who is likely to develop serious depression in response to loss, rather than simply passing through a period of mourning, can be thought of as someone who has no abiding sense of his own worth, and who therefore has no inner resources to fall back upon when loss or deprivation assails him. Such a person remains entirely dependent upon external supplies to keep up his self-esteem; upon other people to love or admire him, or upon achievement to boost his ego. We think it probable that a child who has received the kind of irrational praise and adoration which loving parents habitually extend, gradually acquires a built-in sense of its own worth which may be unjustified in objective terms, but which becomes a source of inner strength when things go wrong. It is probable that such a process continues throughout the years of childhood rather than being linked especially with the first year of life, as Freud and his associate Karl Abraham believed.

There are a variety of reasons why such a process may not take place, thus leaving the subject especially vulnerable to

57

depression. Perhaps the parents did not want the child, or did not love him. Perhaps they set such high standards that the child always felt that he was found wanting. Or perhaps some genetic factor (and there is good evidence for a genetic factor in cases of recurrent depression) rendered the child incapable of introjecting love and thus developing an inner sense of self-esteem however much love was offered.

Freud's concept of a narcissistic object-choice, that is, of object-choice through identification, is particularly interesting in this context. For 'depressive personalities', as I shall call those who are vulnerable to severe depression, are hungry for approval and anxious to avoid criticism or blame which might plunge them into depression. Their anxiety to please makes them hypersensitive to what others are feeling; a form of adaptation to the other which takes place by means of identification. Habitually fitting in with what others are feeling to this extent necessarily involves the suppression or repression of the depressive person's own opinions and feelings; more especially, the assertive or aggressive side of his personality.

Freud also had something to say about mania: the opposite state of mind to that of melancholia, but its well-recognized alternate in cases of manic-depressive psychosis or bipolar affective disorder, as it is often called today. Freud thought that states of 'joy, exultation or triumph' were the model for mania, and were characterized by the sudden availability of psychical energy which had hitherto been used for something else. An analogy might be suddenly taking off the brakes of an automobile, or, to use one of Freud's own examples, 'when a long and arduous struggle is finally crowned with success'. Whereas in states of depression, the subject reproaches himself for his shortcomings, in states of mania the individual not only appears to be well pleased with himself, but may attribute to himself almost magical powers; the 'omnipotence' which Freud thought characteristic of the infant's supposed state of primary narcissism. Freud considered that, in mania, the split between the ego-ideal and the ego was abolished. The super-ego, therefore, no longer concerned itself with pointing out in what ways the ego fell short of the ego-ideal, since there was no longer any division between the two entities.

> On the basis of our analysis of the ego it cannot be doubted that in cases of mania the ego and the ego ideal have fused together, so that the person, in a mood of triumph and self-satisfaction, disturbed by no self-criticism, can enjoy the abolition of his inhibitions, his feelings of consideration for others, and his self-reproaches (*SE*, XVIII.132).

We commented earlier on the accuracy of Freud's description of severe depression, a variety of mental illness which may require admission to hospital but which, nevertheless, is often encountered in private practice. Freud's notes on states of mania are both briefer and less satisfactory, probably because he had little actual experience of the condition. Manic patients are rare in private psychiatric practice because they seldom seek medical help for themselves. They are admitted to mental hospitals and clinics either because their relatives arrange this, or because they behave antisocially and have to be restrained. Manic patients seldom exhibit the unmixed states of 'joy, exultation or triumph' which Freud described. In addition, they are usually irritable, aggressive, and distractible. Although mild states of hypomania are agreeable, and may include a rapid flow of ideas leading to intense creativity, the majority of manic patients are over-excited rather than happy, and, after recovery, describe their experience as intensely disturbing rather than joyful.

It is often forgotten that Freud had very little experience of patients suffering from severe mental illness. In 1885, while waiting to hear whether or not he had obtained a grant to study with Charcot in Paris, Freud worked as a locum tenens for three weeks in a private mental hospital in Oberdöbling on the outskirts of Vienna. He described the inmates to his fiancée as 'a mixture of feeble-minded and eccentric'. Apart from his period of work with Charcot at the Salpêtrière, which was chiefly concerned with hysteria, this three weeks at Oberdöbling was the sum of Freud's clinical experience with psychotic in-patients. As we shall see, his famous study of the paranoid Judge Schreber was based upon the patient's writings rather than upon any actual encounter with him. In his introduction to that study, Freud states that, like other psychiatrists, he sees 'plenty of cases of paranoia and of dementia praecox' (schizophrenia); but as Freud considered such cases unsuitable for psycho-analysis, he makes no claim to have studied them deeply. Jung worked as a psychiatrist in the Burghölzli mental hospital from 1900 to 1909 before giving up his post in favour of private practice. If Freud had had a similarly long experience of working closely with patients suffering from chronic schizophrenia, manic-depressive psychosis, and other forms of severe mental illness, he might have constructed a psychopathology based upon psychosis rather than upon neurosis. Such a psychopathology would probably be more concerned with the development of the individual's sense of reality than with the vicissitudes of his infantile sexuality. Freud's causal explanations of psychotic states are too narrowly based to satisfy most psychiatrists, but, as always, contain original clinical observations of great interest. The paper on the memoirs of Judge Daniel Paul Schreber referred to above is a telling example of both the acuity and the limitations of Freud's thinking.

Paranoid mental illnesses, of which there are several varieties, are principally characterized by the patient developing delusions of persecution. That is, he supposes that he is being pursued, attacked, poisoned, or injured by someone or some group of people with malign intentions. Very often, these beliefs are accompanied by a grandiose conviction of the sufferer's own importance, which may partly account for his being the subject of so much unwelcome attention. Perhaps he is really of royal descent, or possesses some vital secret which his foes are anxious to extract from him.

Schreber was an unusual case in several respects. Most paranoid psychoses are chronic rather than episodic, but Schreber had an initial mental illness lasting from October 1884 to June 1885 from which he made a good recovery. He returned to his profession as a judge, and remained well until 1893. At the age of 51, shortly after being promoted, he

Aggression, depression, and paranoia

relapsed, became severely mentally ill, and had to remain in hospital until December 1902. His memoirs were published a year after his discharge. He never fully recovered from this second illness. In 1907 he was again admitted to a mental hospital in which he died on 14 April 1911.

During his second illness, Schreber believed that his body was being handled in all kinds of revolting ways, and that he was being persecuted and injured, especially by Professor Flechsig, the director of the clinic in which he was first confined. In time, Schreber's acute mental illness subsided, to be replaced by a chronic delusional system. Like other sufferers from paranoia, Schreber appeared perfectly normal unless the subject-matter of his delusions was touched upon. He obtained his release from hospital in 1902 in spite of the acknowledged persistence of his delusional system which was summarized as follows:

He believed that he had a mission to redeem the world and to restore it to its lost state of bliss. This, however, he could only bring about if he were first transformed from a man into a woman (*SE*, XII.16).

In his own writings, Schreber announced his conviction that, when transformed into a woman, he would be impregnated by divine rays so that a new race of men might be created.

We do not know the content of Schreber's first illness; but Freud's interpretation of his second illness is that it was related to Schreber's fear of, and wish for, sexual relations with Flechsig.

The exciting cause of his illness, then, was an outburst of homosexual libido; the object of this libido was probably from the very first his doctor, Flechsig; and his struggles against the libidinal impulse produced the conflict which gave rise to the symptoms (*SE*, XII.43).

Freud goes on to interpret Schreber's presumed homosexual feelings towards his psychiatrist as a transference of earlier unconscious homosexual feelings which had originally been directed towards his father. The later substitution of God as impregnator for Flechsig as persecutor is traced back to a similar source. Freud states that

> the familiar principal forms of paranoia can all be represented as contradictions of the single proposition: '*I* (a man) *love him* (a man)', and indeed that they exhaust all the possible ways in which such contradictions could be formulated.
>
> (*SE*, XII.63)

Freud explains delusions of persecution by affirming that the patient's denial of his homosexual feelings first takes the form 'I do not *love* him – I *hate* him'; and second becomes transformed by projection into '*He hates* (persecutes) *me*, which will justify me in hating him.' Freud is convinced that the persecutor is always a person of the same sex who was once loved.

Freud made much of the fact that Schreber's father was a well-known physician and pedagogue whose views on physical education were widely recognized. He had died at the early age of 53 when Schreber himself was 19. Freud defends his interpretation that Schreber's delusions about God were ultimately derived from his feelings about his father by pointing out that such an eminent man would be even more likely than most fathers to arouse those feelings of 'reverent submission and mutinous insubordination' which Freud considered characteristic of boys' infantile attitudes towards their fathers.

Although Freud took the trouble to identify Judge Schreber's father as Dr Daniel Gottlob Moritz Schreber, and also to discover that Judge Schreber had an elder brother, he did not go any further in attempting to find out what Judge Schreber's childhood was actually like or what manner of man his father really was. Had he done so, he would have discovered that Dr Schreber was an authoritarian monster. His elder son shot himself at the age of 38; his younger son, Judge Schreber, became psychotic in the way described above. Lack of space prevents discussion of Dr Schreber's insistence on breaking a child's will, on keeping the child's body absolutely straight with various restrictive devices, on his use of enemas to prevent nocturnal emissions, and other horrors. A full account of them can be found in Morton Schatzman's book *Soul Murder* (New York, 1973).

In Chapter 2 I referred to the fact that Freud's insistence upon the persistence or recrudescence of infantile sexual phantasies as the causal agents of neurosis had sometimes encouraged psycho-analysts to neglect the real events and circumstances which influence people's lives. Freud's own failure to discover anything about Schreber's father is a striking example of this.

Freud does attempt to give an explanation of why Schreber's second illness should have occurred when he was 51. Freud assumes an increased liability to illness in both men and women at this 'climacteric' period. He also points out that Schreber had lost his father and brother, and that he had had no children; more especially no sons 'upon whom he could have drained off his unsatisfied homosexual affections'. And so Schreber resuscitates the feminine wishes which Freud assumes that he had had towards his father in early childhood.

Freud's contention that paranoia is based upon conflicts concerning homosexual impulses has inspired a great deal of research. Fisher and Greenberg, in their review of this literature, conclude that experimental investigations do on the whole support the idea that 'paranoids and nonparanoids respond significantly differently to stimuli with homosexual connotations'. However, Freud's contention that the persecutor is always of the same sex as the subject is not confirmed.

During the acute phase of his illness, Schreber, like many other sufferers from similar illnesses, thought that a great catastrophe was imminent, perhaps the end of the world. After he had recovered sufficiently to be discharged from hospital, Schreber still believed that a catastrophe had happened, but realized, at any rate in part, that the disaster had been within himself rather than in the external world. Freud postulates that, in the acute stage of his illness, the paranoic's world has indeed come to an end, since he is unable any longer to maintain his emotional ties with it. The mechanism of projection makes him perceive this as pertaining to the external world rather than to himself. Subsequently, he constructs a new world based upon his delusional system. Freud makes the penetrating observation that a delusional system of this kind should be regarded as 'an attempt at recovery, a process of reconstruction'. At a time when the delusions of the insane were usually dismissed as pathological nonsense rather than as phenomena requiring investigation and understanding, Freud's remarks were startlingly original.

The paper on Schreber tells us a great deal about Freud's processes of thought and method of interpretation. It shows how important it is, in considering Freud's work, to sift the wheat from the chaff. Freud's comments on the course of Schreber's illness, on jealousy, on projection, and on the positive functions of delusional systems are often illuminating. But his failure to relate Schreber's character structure and the content of his delusions to the easily ascertained, dire paternal system in which he had been reared is a serious omission. And can anyone really suppose that the emergence of homosexual phantasies in middle life can be regarded as a sufficient cause for the outbreak of a psychotic illness of such severity? Even at the turn of the nineteenth century, an intelligent, educated judge, well used to the world and its ways, would hardly be unaware that men and women have a variety of sexual thoughts and phantasies which they might not like to acknowledge publicly but which are unlikely to be so shocking that they send them mad. Krafft-Ebing's *Psychopathia Sexualis*, with its wealth of information about every kind of sexual perversion, had been published in 1886. Sexuality and its variants were a contemporary topic of discussion in Vienna.

Freud's insistence that the persistence of infantile sexual phantasy was the root cause of mental illness has seldom been less convincingly displayed than in the case of Schreber. Even if all paranoid patients show a particular interest in, or aversion from, homosexual themes when psychologically tested, it does not follow that unresolved homosexual conflicts are the sole cause of paranoid mental illnesses. It is far more likely that this preoccupation is part of a much more profound and general disorder.

7 Jokes and *The Psycho-Pathology of Everyday Life*

The first part of this book has been chiefly concerned with Freud's investigation of the psycho-pathology of the neuroses and psychoses, because this formed the springboard from which psycho-analysis took off in its attempt to become a comprehensive psychology. As indicated in Chapter 1, Freud made speculative theoretical incursions into other fields from the earliest days of psycho-analysis. Had he confined himself to the study of the various forms of mental illness, psycho-analysis would hardly have exerted so wide an influence; but Freud was convinced that his discoveries about human motivation and the unconscious applied not only to neurotics but to every human endeavour.

The Psycho-Pathology of Everyday Life became one of Freud's most popular books. It is concerned with the famous 'Freudian slip'; that is, with slips of the tongue, slips of the pen, faulty recall of names, forgetting of intentions, and other errors. Freud strives to support his belief that all mental events are causally determined by demonstrating that such mistakes or 'parapraxes' are the result of interference by repressed, unconscious thoughts. A case reported by Jung will serve as a simple example.

A Herr Y. fell in love with a lady; but he met with no success, and shortly afterwards she married a Herr X. Thereafter, Herr Y., in spite of having known Herr X. for a long time and even having business dealings with him, forgot his name over and over again, so that several times he had to enquire what it was from other people when he wanted to correspond with Herr X. (*SE*, VI.25).

Obviously, his resentment of his successful rival made Y. want to ignore X.'s existence.

It is equally easy to interpret the following example of a slip of the pen:

> An American living in Europe who had left his wife on bad terms felt that he could now effect a reconciliation with her, and asked her to come across the Atlantic and join him on a certain date. 'It would be fine', he wrote, 'if you could come on the *Mauretania* as I did'. He did not however dare to send the sheet of paper which had this sentence on it. He preferred to write it out again. For he did not want her to notice how he had to correct the name of the ship. He had first written *Lusitania* (*SE*, VI.121–2).

The *Lusitania* was sunk off the coast of Ireland by a German submarine during the First World War.

Not all Freud's examples are equally straightforward. Some of his interpretations seem tortuous and contrived. As we noted when discussing dreams, Freud used considerable ingenuity when it was needed to support his theories. The very first example which he gives is a case in point. Freud found himself unable to remember the name of the artist who had painted some famous frescos in Orvieto cathedral. Instead of the correct name, 'Signorelli', the names of two other painters, Botticelli and Boltraffio, kept on occurring to him. Freud's explanation of this piece of forgetfulness occupies four pages of text and includes his reluctance to talk to a stranger about sex, his wish to forget the suicide of a former patient, and an account of how his repressed thoughts caused the name Signorelli to be split into two, while at the same time substituting the German 'Herr' for the Italian 'Signor'. 'Herr' is taken from Herzegovina, and the 'Bo' of Botticelli and Boltraffio from Bosnia. Herzegovina and Bosnia were occupied by the Turks, about whose sexual customs Freud was reluctant to talk to a mere acquaintance. While staying at Trafoi, Freud had heard the disturbing news of his former patient's suicide. Trafoi therefore contributes to his error of recall by furnishing part of the name 'Boltraffio'. Freud is trying to establish that two topics he had wished to avoid nevertheless manifested themselves in the names which substituted themselves for the name he had forgotten. It is the same kind of interpretation which he applied to obsessional rituals; namely, that the ritual is an indirect expression of an instinctual impulse which the sufferer had repressed and which therefore could not be discharged in a straightforward manner.

Freud's explanation is extremely ingenious; both difficult to fault and yet in the end unconvincing. It seems 'too clever by half' as do many of Freud's dream interpretations; an attribution to unconscious mental activity of over-elaborate means to conceal the essentially trivial. Many slips of the tongue and instances of forgetting are undoubtedly motivated in the ways suggested by Freud; but this may not be true of all. For example, most elderly people find the retrieval of names increasingly difficult. Names may be accurately registered, but it takes longer and longer to recall them. In Chapter 3 we doubted whether Freud was right in attributing infantile amnesia entirely to repression, and suggested alternative explanations. Similar doubts apply to Freud's theory of adult forgetting. For instance, Freud does not consider the social context in which the failure of memory takes place, nor the possibility that names may be originally registered with different degrees of intensity according to circumstances. One is more likely to recall the name of a new acquaintance with whom one has spent an evening than that of a person to whom one has been briefly introduced at a party. But, having decided that unconscious wishes and thoughts cause interference with recall in some instances, Freud makes the generalization that this must be so in every case.

Sebastiano Timpanaro wrote a book *The Freudian Slip* in which he criticized Freud for not taking into account that many slips are the kind of errors with which all writers are familiar: repeating words one has just used; omitting words because one's thought leaps ahead of one's pen, and so on. In his review of the book, the psycho-analyst Charles Rycroft adds a criticism that was first made by Jung in connection with free association. Many of Freud's interpretations of errors depend upon his obtaining the subject's associations to the circumstances surrounding the error. To be sure, Freud quickly reaches disturbing material by this means; not always sexual material, as one would expect from Freud's theories, but thoughts of jealousy, personal advancement, prejudice, or hostility which are unacceptable to the person furnishing the associations. As anyone who has honestly experimented with free association knows, the technique inevitably and rapidly brings to mind topics about which one is emotionally concerned. As Rycroft points out, 'the eventual arrival at "significant material" is not therefore evidence that the starting-point was in any sense caused by it'.

Freud's other early excursion from the consulting room into everyday life is concerned with humour. *Jokes and their Relation to the Unconscious* was first published in 1905. Freud had started to collect Jewish jokes as early as 1897; but his interest in the subject gained impetus when his friend Fliess, on reading the proofs of *The Interpretation of Dreams*, complained that dreams were too full of jokes. In his reply to Fliess's letter, Freud writes:

> All dreamers are equally insufferably witty, and they need to be because they are under pressure and the direct route is barred to them. . . . The ostensible wit of all unconscious processes is intimately related to the theory of the joke and the comic (*The Freud-Fliess Letters*, 371).

Freud wrote so clearly and persuasively that, even in translation, most of his work is a pleasure to read. The book on jokes is an exception. This is partly because jokes suffer grievously in translation, and partly because explaining jokes annihilates their humour.

Freud analyses what he calls the *technique* of jokes, and points out that some of the mechanisms employed are indeed to be found in dreams; in particular, condensation, and the substitution of one word for another. An English example is Disraeli's remark that old people are inclined to fall into their 'anecdotage', thus condensing 'anecdote' and 'dotage'. A similar example is a reference to the Christmas season as 'alcoholidays'. Freud goes on to list other mechanisms which appear in dreams and also in jokes: 'displacement, faulty reasoning, absurdity, indirect representation, representation by the opposite'. He then proceeds to classify jokes into two main classes: 'innocent' jokes and 'tendentious' jokes. The former are solely dependent upon verbal ingenuity; the latter upon the indirect expression of hostility or obscenity. It is the tendentious jokes which chiefly interest Freud. Indeed, as we shall see, he is hard put to it to explain why 'innocent' jokes give us such pleasure. No such difficulty attaches to the interpretation of 'tendentious' jokes. They easily fall into line with neurotic symptoms, slips of the tongue, and dreams.

> And here at last we can understand what it is that jokes achieve in the service of their purpose. They make possible the satisfaction of an instinct (whether lustful or hostile) in the face of an obstacle that stands in its way. They circumvent this obstacle and in that way draw pleasure from a source which the obstacle had made inaccessible.
>
> (*SE*, VII.100–1)

The obstacle may be either an internal inhibition or else social; that is, the presence of a person who might be shocked. In this early work, Freud is already picturing civilization as the enemy of instinct and an instigator of repression. Tendentious jokes are a way of bypassing the barriers against the direct expression of both obscenity and aggression which civilization has set up.

When considering Freud's interpretation of manic states in Chapter 6, we noted that he thought that states of 'joy, exultation or triumph' were characterized by the sudden availability of psychical energy, and we compared this with releasing the brakes of a car. The pleasure accompanying a joke is, Freud believed, of a similar nature. It is easy to see this in the case of a tendentious joke in which the joker, by dressing up his obscene thoughts or aggressive impulses in humorous guise, is circumventing his own internal inhibitions. But Freud also acknowledged that purely external factors, rather than internal inhibitions, might prevent the direct expression of such impulses. Freud quotes as an example of what he means the familiar story of the royal personage who sees a man in the crowd who closely resembles himself:

'Was your mother at one time in service in the Palace?'
'No, your Highness, but my father was.'

By making a joke, the man can express aggression toward the high and mighty prince which, because of the latter's power, he could not do directly. In this case, Freud affirmed that the pleasure obtained from the joke was because no barrier against expressing the man's true feelings had to be erected.

> The cases of an external and an internal obstacle differ only in the fact that in the latter an already existing inhibition is lifted and that in the former the erection of a new one is avoided. That being so, we shall not be relying too much on speculation if we assert that both for erecting and for maintaining a psychical inhibition some 'psychical expenditure' is required. And, since we know that in both cases of the use of tendentious jokes pleasure is obtained, it is therefore plausible to suppose that *this yield of pleasure corresponds to the psychical expenditure that is saved* (*SE*, VIII.118).

This piece of ingenuity was necessary because Freud wanted an explanation which would apply to 'innocent' jokes as well as to tendentious ones. Innocent jokes depend upon verbal felicities, puns, play upon words, combining incongruous words, and so on. Freud writes of being 'driven to conclude that the techniques of jokes are themselves sources of pleasure', as if he was reluctant to admit that anything other than instinctual release could be pleasurable. Freud resolves his problem by postulating that the pleasure obtained from innocent jokes is also that of economy. When we rediscover something familiar, as often happens in jokes, or when we link together by verbal association two things which are not at first sight congruous, we are playing with words, avoiding the effort of critical thought, and by thus economizing our expenditure of psychic energy, obtaining pleasure.

Freud calls this minor pleasure deriving from economy a 'fore-pleasure', thus comparing it with the various fore-pleasures characteristic of sexual arousal, in which stimulation of parts of the body other than the genitals leads on to the real thing, involvement of the genitals themselves. For, finally, Freud disposes of the problem posed by the 'innocent' joke by alleging that:

> Jokes, even if the thought contained in them is non-tendentious and thus only serves theoretical intellectual interests, are in fact never non-tendentious (*SE*, VIII.132).

> The originally non-tendentious joke, which began as play, is *secondarily* brought into relation with purposes from which nothing that takes form in the mind can ultimately keep away (*SE*, VIII.133).

Freud states that a good joke makes a total impression; that it is often difficult to know whether pleasure is principally derived from the form of the joke, or from the thought contained in it. He thinks of form as a kind of wrapping which makes the underlying thought more acceptable, like sugar coating a pill. As we shall see, Freud uses the same analogy when discussing works of art. He writes of aesthetic form as a device by which artists both conceal their 'egoistic day-dreams' and also render them more acceptable to other people. In both cases, Freud is denying that true pleasure can be derived from form. Any pleasure which we get from the verbal ingenuity of a joke, or from the aesthetic order imposed by an artist, must be minor; a 'fore-pleasure' as opposed to a final pleasure, which must, in Freud's view, be sensual. This is not contradicted by Freud's recognition that tendentious jokes allow for the expression of aggression as well as sex since, at the time he was writing, he still regarded aggression as constituting a sadistic aspect of the sexual instinct.

What is perhaps surprising is Freud's failure to acknowledge that there is such a thing as pleasure in the exercise of power or mastery. When discussing play in this same book, Freud refers to a writer called C. Groos who, in his book on games, refers to 'joy in power' or joy in overcoming a difficulty. Freud at once dismisses this as secondary. Yet, we must surely accept that pleasure is to be obtained from exercising a skill, whether the skill be physical or mental. Jokes are usually variants upon some well-worn theme; but we do not object to this if the joke itself displays verbal ingenuity and economy of construction. In other words, what we appreciate, even in an obviously tendentious joke, is its form as much as its content. The form of the joke is not simply a bribe, an 'incentive bonus', as Freud calls it, but an essential part of what gives rise to pleasure. If we make a new joke, we are pleased with our own cleverness. If we hear a new joke, we appreciate the cleverness of its creator. The joke is concerned with form; with imposing an order upon material by linking incongruities. It is therefore an aesthetic product, albeit of a primitive variety.

The search for order, for explanatory principles, for common features which link disparate things together is an inescapable human endeavour. Freud himself, when he had solved a problem which had been perplexing him, must have known the pleasure which accompanies the 'eureka' experience. Yet he continued to regard such a pleasure as a sublimation, not as primary. As late as 1930, Freud wrote:

A satisfaction of this kind, such as an artist's joy in creating, in giving his phantasies body, or a scientist's in solving problems or discovering truths, has a special quality which we shall certainly one day be able to characterize in meta-psychological terms. At present we can only say figuratively that such satisfactions seem 'finer and higher'. But their intensity is mild as compared with that derived from the sating of crude and primary instinctual impulses; it does not convulse our physical being (*SE*, XXI.79–80).

In the next chapter, we shall review what Freud had to say about art and artists.

8 Art and literature

During the twentieth century, psycho-analysis has had a major effect upon both art and literature. Freud's concept of the unconscious, his use of free association, and his rediscovery of the importance of dreams encouraged painters, sculptors, and writers to experiment with the fortuitous and the irrational, to pay serious attention to their inner worlds of dream and day-dream, and to find significance in thoughts and images which they would previously have dismissed as absurd or illogical. Such movements as Dadaism and Surrealism owe much to Freud; and so do those works of literature which, like Virginia Woolf's *The Waves*, depend upon the employment of 'stream-of-consciousness' techniques. After psycho-analysis became established, biographers began to feel that, unless they had managed to uncover the emotional influences to which their subjects had been exposed during the earliest years of childhood, their portraits were incomplete. Revelations about sexual behaviour and preferences became almost obligatory, since Freud had laid it down that sexuality was the central driving force in human nature. It became generally accepted that even such figures as politicians could not be fully understood unless the psycho-analytic spotlight was brought to bear upon them. Freud himself collaborated with the American diplomat William C. Bullitt in writing a psycho-analytic study of Woodrow Wilson, the twenty-eighth President of the United States. Although a number of reputable historians have found psycho-analytic concepts valuable in understanding historical characters, this particular book has been generally regarded as disastrous, since both Freud and Bullitt were heavily pre-judiced against Wilson. For example, they call him 'a prime prig'; and go on to write: 'Sickly, spectacled, shy, guarded by father, mother and sisters, Tommy Wilson never had a fist fight in his life', as if having fist fights was a *sine qua non* of masculinity. They also pour scorn upon his religious beliefs and accuse him of identifying himself with Christ. This tendentious biography is an early example of using psycho-analysis as 'character assassination'.

Freud himself displayed a curiously ambivalent attitude to art and artists. As we noted in Chapter 1, he had a deep knowledge of, and love for, literature, which manifests itself in the elegance of his own writing. He was also responsive to sculpture and, in lesser degree, to painting. He himself wrote that he was almost incapable of obtaining pleasure from music. Freud wrote a number of books and papers on art and artists, of which the most famous are *Delusions and Dreams in Jensen's 'Gradiva'*; *Leonardo de Vinci and a Memory of his Childhood*; 'The Moses of Michelangelo'; and 'Dostoevsky and Parricide'.

Freud believed that sublimation of unsatisfied libido was responsible for producing all art and literature. That is, he thought that artists discharged their infantile sexuality by con-verting it into non-instinctual forms. As we saw in Chapter 3, Freud had suggested that repression of perverse, pre-genital components of the sexual instinct was responsible for the arrest of sexual development and consequent lack of sexual satisfaction which he regularly found in neurotics. If the impulses were not repressed, but for one reason or another exaggerated, the person concerned might become a sexual pervert rather than a neurotic.

A third way of dealing with the same material is open to those who are artistically gifted. Artists, in this view, are people who may avoid neurosis and perversion by sublimating their impulses in their work. Freud did not attempt to explain the nature of the artist's gift, any more than he tried to explain manual dexterity, intelligence, or any other of the cognitive and perceptual differences between people which experimental psychologists study. What Freud was concerned with was motivation; and in his view motivation, ultimately, could be derived only from the death instinct manifesting itself as aggression, or from the sexual instinct. Moreover, in the Freudian scheme, motivation had to be traced back to instinc-tual repressions in the earliest years of childhood. The limita-tions of such a view of 'instinct' are clearly demonstrable in

Freud's writings on art and artists. As we noted at the end of the last chapter, Freud did not admit that the human need to order our experience and make sense of it was anything but a secondary phenomenon, since it could not be directly linked with the pleasure principle. Yet both art and science, although very different types of human endeavour, are concerned with seeking order in complexity and unity in diversity; and the impulse to do this, which is biologically adaptive, could equally well be regarded as 'instinctive'.

This limitation meant that Freud abandoned any interest he may have had in the *form* of a work of art, and paid attention only to its *content*. He modestly admits as much in his paper on 'The Moses of Michelangelo'.

> I may say at once that I am no connoisseur in art, but simply a layman. I have often observed that the subject-matter of works of art has a stronger attraction for me than their formal and technical qualities, though to the artist their value lies first and foremost in these latter. I am unable rightly to appreciate many of the methods used and the effects obtained in art (*SE*, XIII.211).

Since content, rather than style, was the problem to which Freud addressed himself, it was natural that he should apply the same technique of interpretation to works of art as he did to dreams, phantasies, and neurotic symptoms. Granted his assumption that art is a sublimation, what he could do and did, with varying success, was to discover in the work of art evidence of the artist's presumed infantile conflicts.

Freud's essay on Leonardo da Vinci illustrates both the insights and the limitations of this approach. It is known from historical sources that Leonardo was homosexually inclined and also that he was an illegitimate child. During the course of the same year in which he was born, his father married another woman. His mother also married soon after the child's birth. Leonardo was later adopted by his father and brought up in his father's household. There is no historical record which indicates what kind of relationship Leonardo may have had with his mother or his stepmother, or which tells us what kind of people they were. Nor is it known at what age Leonardo was removed from his mother to be brought up by his stepmother and father; although it is recorded that he was part of that household by the time he was 5 years old.

Freud analyses a childhood recollection recorded by Leonardo in which he claimed that, while in his cradle, a large bird opened his mouth with its tail and struck him many times with its tail against his lips. Freud reasonably supposes that this is so unlikely to have happened in reality that it is probably a later phantasy of Leonardo's which he transposed to early childhood. As might be expected, Freud interprets the phantasy as being an expression of passive homosexuality; the bird's tail substituting for the penis, and the wish to take the penis in the mouth being ultimately derived from the experience of suckling, which Freud calls 'the first source of pleasure in our life'.

But why is the mother represented by a bird? Freud, assuming that the bird is a vulture, expounds the connection between mothers and vultures in Egyptian mythology. He claims that Leonardo chose this bird to represent his mother because vultures were supposed to be of the female sex only, and a vulture would therefore be a particularly appropriate image of the mother in the case of a child who lacked a father.

Unfortunately, Freud's interpretation is based upon a mistranslation. The bird was not a vulture, but a kite. Whereas vultures can be shown to have mythological connections with the mother, kites cannot. Moreover, although he admits that we have no actual record of when Leonardo was taken into his father's household, Freud goes on to affirm that the phantasy indicates that he must have spent his earliest years with his 'poor forsaken, real mother, so that he had time to feel the absence of his father'.

One cannot blame the art historians for dismissing Freud's interpretation as totally unjustified; but, as so often with Freud, there is wheat to be found among the chaff. Freud comments at length upon the famous picture *Virgin and Child with St Anne*. St Anne is represented as being scarcely older than her daughter, the Virgin Mary. Freud supposes that the subject of mother, grandmother and child, which is rarely chosen by painters, may have occurred to Leonardo because his father's household included his paternal grandmother as well as his stepmother. He goes on to suggest that the similarity in age between the two women in the picture may be a reflection of the fact that Leonardo in effect had two mothers: his real mother and his stepmother.

This speculation seems both more interesting and more legitimate. The subjects which an artist portrays, and the ways in which he chooses to present them, are often determined by his patrons and by the conventions of his time. But they are also bound to reflect something of his own personality and personal history, although he himself may be unaware of any such connection. Whether the subjects chosen are anything to do with repressed infantile sexual phantasies is more dubious.

Freud estimated Dostoevsky's literary standing as 'not far behind Shakespeare', and considered *The Brothers Karamazov* 'the most magnificent novel ever written'. He justifiably claims that Dostoevsky's depiction of so many violent, egotistical and murderous characters points to similar tendencies within the novelist himself, and refers to his possible confession of a sexual assault upon a young girl. Dostoevsky's friend and biographer Strakhov refers to this in a letter to Tolstoy, and there is also a story that Dostoevsky confessed it to Turgenev. The subject appears in Dostoevsky's writings more than once. Freud also draws attention to the sado-masochistic traits which Dostoevsky undoubtedly displayed, and to his compulsive gambling. Freud's interpretation of Dostoevsky's psychopathology rests chiefly upon the supposition that Dr Dostoevsky, the novelist's father, was 'especially violent'. He assumes that Dostoevsky's disposition was rooted in an unresolved conflict between masculine (sadistic) revolt and feminine (masochistic) submission in relation to his father, and that the severity of Dostoevsky's self-punitive conscience was derived from his father's punitiveness. Freud wrote:

Thus the formula for Dostoevsky is as follows: a person with a specially strong innate bisexual disposition, who can defend himself with special intensity against dependence on a specially severe father (*SE*, XXI.185).

In reality, although Dr Dostoevsky was strict in insisting that his children devoted themselves to study from an early age, he was a particularly conscientious father who gave an unusual amount of his time to his children's education, who never employed physical punishment himself, and who sent his children to private schools in order to avoid having them beaten although he could scarcely afford the expense.

As Joseph Frank demonstrates in his definitive biography of Dostoevsky, Freud read a footnote in a biography published in 1883 which hinted at 'a very peculiar piece of evidence about the illness of Feodor Mihailovich which relates to his earliest youth and connects it with a tragic event in their family life'. Although there is nothing about either punishment or father in this passage, Freud recalls what he read in a letter to Stefan Zweig as:

Somewhere in a biography of D. I was shown a passage which traced back the later affliction of the man to the boy's having been punished by the father under very serious circumstances.

This is an instance of Freud unwittingly distorting his recollection in order to support the view of Dostoevsky's psychopathology which he had already constructed; a wish-fulfilling phantasy determining faulty recall in the way described in *The Psycho-Pathology of Everyday Life*. The illness or 'later affliction' referred to is Dostoevsky's epilepsy. On this 'evidence', Freud concludes that Dostoevsky's fits were almost certainly not true epilepsy, but were caused by emotional conflict rather than by brain damage. He also assumes that Dostoevsky had 'attacks' in childhood which foreshadowed his later epilepsy and which were characterized by fears of death and sudden states of lethargy. Joseph Frank conclusively demonstrates that neither symptom occurred during Dostoevsky's childhood, but dated from the years 1846 to 1847, when Dostoevsky would have been 25 years old.

Dostoevsky's father was said to have been murdered by his serfs when Dostoevsky was a student of 18. Freud interprets Dostoevsky's epilepsy, whether 'true' epilepsy or not, as a masochistic desire for self-punishment, and states that it began on hearing of the death of his father. In fact, all the evidence, with the exception of one unsupported 'family tradition' recorded by his daughter, suggests that Dostoevsky's first epileptic attack occurred in 1850, when he was in a prison camp in Siberia. The medical reports strongly suggest that he suffered from typical 'grand mal' convulsions (that is, 'true' epilepsy); and this is further borne out by the fact that his son Aleksey died of epilepsy at the age of 3, since there is evidence of a hereditary factor in epilepsy.

Enough of Joseph Frank's detailed indictment of Freud's guesswork has been quoted to demonstrate that, once Freud had come to a conclusion, it was so difficult for him to modify it that he was not above selecting only that 'evidence' which supported his suppositions. One cannot help being reminded of his failure to discover the true nature of Judge Schreber's father. It must be recorded that Joseph Frank has no particular animus against Freud. Although sceptical about Freud's interpretation of Dostoevsky's character, he had assumed that Freud had based his interpretation upon accurate data. It was only when he studied the events of Dostoevsky's early life in detail that he found Freud to be unreliable at the purely factual level.

Freud's paper 'The Moses of Michelangelo' is in a different category. There are no speculations about Michelangelo's early childhood, and no interpretations of his psychopathology. Instead there is a learned and detailed review of what art historians have written about this particular statue, combined with Freud's own deductions about the meaning of the pose which the artist has chosen. Anyone reading this essay will be impressed with the acuteness of Freud's scrutiny, his attention to detail, and the modesty of his claims. Whether or not modern art historians agree with Freud's interpretation of the statue as

> a concrete expression of the highest mental achievement
> that is possible in a man, that of struggling successfully
> against an inward passion for the sake of a cause to which he
> has devoted himself (*SE*, XIII.233)

hardly matters. The essay reflects both Freud's learning and his
considerable powers of observation. It is ironic that his best
paper on art and artists should be one in which psycho-analytic
theory scarcely figures.

As indicated at the beginning of this chapter, Freud considered that art and literature were produced by sublimation of
unsatisfied libido. Although Freud considered that sublimation
was necessarily employed by normal people living under the
constraints imposed by civilization, the implication of Freud's
view must be that, if libido was fully discharged, art and
literature would not be necessary. It also follows that, since
artists devote so much of their time to activities which are the
product of sublimation, they must be closer to being neurotic
than the average person. This, indeed, was Freud's view.

> An artist is once more in rudiments an introvert, not far
> removed from neurosis. He is oppressed by excessively
> powerful instinctual needs. He desires to win honour, power,
> wealth, fame and the love of women; but he lacks the means
> for achieving these satisfactions. Consequently, like any
> other unsatisfied man, he turns away from reality and
> transfers all his interest, and his libido too, to the wishful
> constructions of his life of phantasy, whence the path might
> lead to neurosis (*SE*, XVI.376).

Freud thought that phantasy was derived from play. In his
view, both play and phantasy involved turning away from, or
denying, reality, and were therefore activities which ought to
be outgrown.

> The growing child, when he stops playing, gives up nothing
> but the link with real objects; instead of *playing*, he now
> *phantasies*. He builds castles in the air and creates what are
> called *day-dreams* (*SE*, IX.145).

The creative writer does the same as the child at play. He creates a world of phantasy which he takes very seriously – that is which he invests with large amounts of emotion – while separating it sharply from reality (*SE*, IX.144).

We may lay it down that a happy person never phantasies, only an unsatisfied one. The motive forces of phantasies are unsatisfied wishes, and every single phantasy is the fulfilment of a wish, a correction of an unsatisfying reality.

(*SE*, IX.146)

Neurotics turn away from reality because they find it unbearable – either the whole or parts of it (*SE*, XII.218).

So play, dreams, and phantasies are linked together as childish, escapist, wish-fulfilling techniques of compensating for an unsatisfying reality.

In Chapter 5 we referred to Freud's distinction between the two varieties of mental functioning which he called 'primary process' and 'secondary process'. The former is governed by wish-fulfilment and the pleasure principle; the latter by conscious planning and the reality principle.

With the introduction of the reality principle one species of thought-activity was split off; it was kept free from reality-testing, and remained subordinated to the pleasure principle alone. This activity is *phantasying*, which begins already in children's play, and later, continued as *day-dreaming*, abandons dependence upon real objects (*SE*, XII.222).

Freud did admit, though only grudgingly, that artists were not merely neurotics who used their gifts to evade reality.

Art brings about a reconciliation between the two principles in a new way. An artist is originally a man who turns away from reality because he cannot come to terms with the renunciation of instinctual satisfaction which it at first demands, and who allows his erotic and ambitious wishes full play in the life of phantasy. He finds a way back to reality, however, from this world of phantasy by making use of special gifts to mould his phantasies into truths of a new kind, which are valued by men as precious reflections of reality (*SE*, XII.224).

This strange conception of art and artist implies that, although the artist may just escape falling into a neurosis, his art is still an indirect way of obtaining instinctual satisfactions which, if he were better adapted to reality, he would either enjoy or else renounce. In other words, art is primarily escapist. In an ideal world in which everyone had matured sufficiently to replace the pleasure principle by the reality principle, there would be no need for art.

This conclusion, coming as it does from a brilliant writer who was deeply appreciative of both literature and the visual arts, will strike most readers as extremely odd. If Freud had lived long enough to become familiar with modern biological thinking, he might have revised his concepts.

For example, ethologists generally agree that play in young animals is not escapist, but adaptive. That is, play facilitates exploration and also, by repetition of movement sequences, encourages the development of muscular skills. Rough-and-tumble play between young animals and young humans is probably an important way of learning the controlled employment of aggression and may also facilitate later sexual fulfilment.

If play is adaptive in the biological sense, may it not be the case that phantasy is also adaptive? There are such things as 'idle' day-dreams which fit Freud's escapist category; but not all phantasies are of this kind. Einstein defined thinking as 'a free play with concepts' and specifically emphasized the need for creative thinking to be free of the constraints imposed by real objects. He could never have conceived the special theory of relativity if he had not employed phantasy, although, of course, the theory had later to be checked by experiment. Freud, as we noted, thought that *The Brothers Karamazov* was the greatest novel ever written. Although the novel originates from Dostoevsky's phantasy, it also contains portraits based upon real people, and, like every great novel, enhances and deepens our understanding of reality rather than providing an escape from it.

In Chapter 4, we found that Freud's theory that dreams were almost invariably hallucinatory fulfilments of repressed wishes would not hold water, and suggested that some dreams were a way of dealing with trauma, whilst others were concerned with processing information. These latter two functions are not escapist, but ways of coming to terms with reality.

Play, phantasy, and the dream, the three activities which Freud linked as escapist wish-fulfilment, can equally well be regarded as adaptive; more especially, as ways of selecting from, and making new combinations of, our inner and outer experience. Freud considered that the motives of the artist and the motives of the scientist could be sharply distinguished. The drive behind the artist's creative activity was unsatisfied libido manifesting itself in escapist phantasy. The drive behind the scientist's activity was to master the external world. What artists do and what scientists do is certainly very different; but, as we have already suggested, both are concerned with creating order, with making sense out of the world and our experience of it, with discovering or fashioning unity from diversity.

Many of the most creative psycho-analysts of recent years, including Rycroft, Winnicott, Bowlby, Marion Milner and Ehrenzweig reject Freud's concept of 'primary process' as archaic, childish, and maladaptive. Phantasy can be escapist, but, when manifest as creative imagination, is a vital aspect of man's adaptation to the world. Goya was surely right when he prefaced his *Caprichos* with this epigraph:

Phantasy abandoned by reason produces impossible monsters; united with reason, it is the mother of the arts and the origin of their marvels.

9 Culture and religion

The application of psycho-analytic theory to anthropology and religion has, on the whole, been disappointing. But Freud's views on these subjects, though not usually accepted by either anthropologists or theologians, are important in demonstrating the way in which psycho-analysis progressed from being a treatment of neurotic illness to being a system of thought which purported to explain almost every human endeavour.

As already indicated, Freud was a highly civilized man himself, but nevertheless regarded civilization as oppressive, since, in his view, it imposed more restraints upon instinctual fulfilment than most human beings could tolerate without developing at least some neurotic symptoms. It is therefore not surprising that Freud was an eager student of primitive and early man; of man as he might have been before civilization had instigated the iron grip of repression. Unfortunately, Freud was writing in the era of 'armchair' anthropology, characterized by extensive theorizing unsupported by evidence from field-work. It was still possible to refer to those belonging to pre-literate cultures as 'savages', and, quite unjustifiably, to equate 'primitive' with 'neurotic' or 'infantile' as Freud did. Today we realize that many so-called primitives may be well adapted to their environment in complex ways; but, before the First World War, Victorian ideas of progress dictated that there had been a clear advance from a 'savage' beginning to the giddy pinnacle of European civilization in the twentieth century. The revelation of the concentration camps and the experience of two world wars have put an end to that kind of complacency.

Totem and Taboo, which consists of four parts originally appearing separately, was first published as a single volume in 1913. Freud's principal sources for his anthropological speculations were Darwin's *The Descent of Man*, Sir James Frazer's *The Golden Bough*, and the theories of Robertson Smith and

J. J. Atkinson. These sources are now partly or wholly discredited.

A totem is a symbolic emblem of a particular social group within a tribe. It may be an animal or, less commonly, a plant or natural phenomenon like rain. A totem is an object of reverence or worship, and is protected by taboos which generally forbid killing it, eating it, or even touching it. On special occasions, however, there may be a ritualized killing and sacramental eating of the totem animal. Allegiance to a particular totem defines social relationships inasmuch as sexual relations between members of the same totem are usually forbidden.

Freud interpreted the totem as representing the father because he knew of three cases in which boys with Oedipal conflicts had phantasies about, or phobias of, animals in which the animal seemed to be a substitute for the father. Freud's own case 'Little Hans' had a fear of being bitten by a horse which Freud believed to have resulted from the repression and subsequent projection of the child's hostility towards his father.

Freud, following Darwin, supposed that primitive man lived in small groups or 'hordes' dominated by a single, powerful male, who not only kept all the females for himself, but also expelled his younger male rivals, thus preventing incest and encouraging the formation of sexual ties outside the original group. Freud went on to suggest that:

> One day the brothers who had been driven out came together, killed and devoured their father and so made an end of the patriarchal horde. . . . The totem meal, which is perhaps man's earliest festival, would thus be a repetition of this memorable and criminal deed, which was the beginning of so many things – of social organization, of moral restrictions and of religion (*SE*, XIII.141–2).

Freud then asserted that the sons who had slaughtered their father became afflicted with such guilt that:

> They revoked their deed by forbidding the killing of the totem, the substitute for their father; and they renounced its fruits by

85

resigning their claim to the women who had now been set free. They thus created out of their filial sense of guilt the two fundamental taboos of totemism, which for that very reason inevitably corresponded to the two repressed wishes of the Oedipus complex. Whoever contravened those taboos became guilty of the only two crimes with which primitive society concerned itself (*SE*, XIII.143).

The ritual totemic meal could be interpreted as a 'return of the repressed'; a temporary symbolic expression of the original impulses of hatred towards the father which guilt usually kept unconscious.

Freud thought that this primal slaughter of the father was a real event which had left 'ineradicable traces in the history of humanity'. In other words, he believed in the discredited Lamarckian hypothesis of the inheritance of acquired characteristics. In spite of his considerable knowledge of Darwin, whose evolutionary theory had displaced Lamarck's idea in the minds of virtually every biologist, Freud obstinately maintained until his death that acquired characteristics could be inherited, and that the origins of religion and morality could indeed be traced back to an actual event.

Freud seems to have been ambivalent about *Totem and Taboo*. On the one hand, he regarded it as a major achievement; on the other, he once said, 'Oh, don't take that seriously—I made that up on a rainy Sunday afternoon.' In reality, there are a number of untenable elements in Freud's theory, in addition to his adherence to Lamarck.

First, there is no evidence from anthropology or from studies of subhuman primates that a 'primal horde' dominated by a single male ever existed. Darwin derived his notion from hearsay reports about the organization of gorilla troops which have since been shown to be false.

Second, totemic meals are rare, and found only in a small minority of tribes professing totemism.

Third, Freud neglects any discussion of the possible importance of the mother in totemic religion; an omission characteristic of psycho-analytic theory, which, until late in its evolution, habitually emphasized the father's role at the expense of that of the mother. This emphasis probably originated from the fact that Freud himself had more problems in his relation to his father than he did in relation to his mother.

Fourth, in at least one of the cases upon which Freud based his theory of the totem representing the father, a quite different interpretation is possible. 'Little Hans', the 5-year-old son of Freud's friend Max Graf, was seen only once by Freud, who treated the child through his father. John Bowlby, re-examining the case, has demonstrated that, like other childhood phobias, Little Hans's phobia is likely to have been caused by fears that his mother would disappear. It has been established that the mother used alarming threats in disciplining Hans, including the threat that she would leave and not come back if Hans were naughty.

In the light of modern anthropology, Darwinian theory, and Bowlby's work on 'attachment', it is easy to be wise after the event and accuse Freud of neglecting evidence to some of which he could not at the time have had access. Nevertheless, *Totem and Taboo* does belong to the wilder shores of speculation, and bears witness to Freud's tendency to generalization from an insufficient basis of fact when he thought that he could thereby find support for psycho-analytic theory. Thomas Mann, in an essay published in 1929, chose *Totem and Taboo* as the work of Freud which had made the strongest impression upon him. This seems bizarre until one realizes that Mann's evaluation is not based upon anthropology, but is entirely literary. Mann wrote that *Totem and Taboo*

is without doubt the one of Freud's productions which has the greatest artistic merit; both in conception and literary form, it is a literary masterpiece allied to, and comparable with, the greatest examples of literary essays.

Some of the same criticisms which have been levelled at *Totem and Taboo* also apply to *Moses and Monotheism*, which was Freud's last completed book, not finished until he was over 80. Freud controversially supposed that Moses, leader and creator of the Jewish people, was originally an Egyptian, as the etymology of his name suggests. The biblical story of Moses records that, in order to avoid the persecution of the Pharaoh, Moses' parents concealed him by the river in an ark of bulrushes, from which he was rescued by the Pharaoh's daughter. Since the princess brought up Moses as her own son, Freud makes the not unreasonable deduction that Moses was in fact her son, and therefore not Jewish in origin. He goes on to suggest that Moses had accepted the revolution of thought instigated by the Pharaoh Akhenaten, who had substituted monotheism for the worship of a multiplicity of gods. When Akhenaten died, a reaction set in threatening monotheistic beliefs. Moses therefore threw in his lot with the oppressed minority of Jews, reinforced their identity by insisting both on monotheism and the practice of circumcision, and finally instituted the Exodus, leading the Jews out of Egypt to discover the promised land. Although the Bible states that Moses died at the age of 120, Freud preferred to believe that Moses was murdered by his people, relying for evidence on a suggestion made by Ernst Sellin, which, when first announced, had been immediately rejected by all other Jewish scholars. Freud eagerly adopted Sellin's hypothesis because it supported his own speculation about parricide and the origins of religion. Freud guessed that the murder of Moses reinforced the inherited sense of guilt dating from the primal parricide described above, and caused a lasting unconscious sense of guilt in the Jewish people.

It is plausible to conjecture that remorse for the murder of Moses provided the stimulus for the wishful phantasy of the Messiah, who was to return and lead his people to redemption and the promised world-dominion (*SE*, XXIII.89).

Moses and Monotheism has been rejected by most critics as one of the least convincing of Freud's writings. As in *Totem and Taboo*, Lamarckian inheritance of acquired characteristics is an integral part of the argument, and there are many historical objections to the book which it would be otiose to catalogue.

It was noted in Chapter 1 that Freud never practised the

Jewish religion. Although he acknowledged that religion might sometimes play a part in suppressing neurotic symptoms, he firmly maintained that religious faith was a wish-fulfilling illusion. In Freud's view, the gods have a threefold task.

> They must exorcize the terrors of nature, they must reconcile men to the cruelty of Fate, particularly as it is shown in death, and they must compensate them for the sufferings which a civilized life in common has imposed on them.
>
> (*SE*, XXI.18)

Freud believed that religion originated in man's feelings of helplessness. As an adult, man is confronted by all manner of dangers, from earthquakes to disease, which threaten him and which he cannot control. As a small child, he was even more helpless, but recognized that his father, however formidable, at least protected him from common dangers.

> The derivation of religious needs from the infant's helplessness and the longing for the father seems to me incontrovertible, especially since the feeling is not simply prolonged from childhood days, but is permanently sustained by fear of the superior power of Fate. I cannot think of any need in childhood as strong as the need for a father's protection (*SE*, XXI.72).

In an earlier paper, Freud had laid more emphasis upon the dangers threatening the individual from within. He noted the similarity between religious practices and obsessional rituals. In his view, obsessional rituals were ways of protecting the ego from the emergence of phantasies, thoughts, or sexual impulses which the individual had repressed; and, at the same time, a displaced and partial expression of those impulses. For example, a patient suffered from the common compulsion to wash his hands frequently; in this case, an expression of guilt about masturbation. In addition, he was compelled to wash each finger separately, thereby making an obscene gesture signifying coitus. Freud considered that religion, as part of civilization, was based on the suppression, the renunciation, of certain instinctual impulses. These impulses, however, are not, as in the neuroses, exclusively components of the sexual instinct; they are self-seeking, socially harmful instincts, though, even so, they are usually not without a sexual component.

(*SE*, IX.125)

Because pious people, in their confessional prayers, acknowledge themselves to be guilty sinners, they need to perform ritual observances as a defence against temptation and as a way of controlling or warding off the instinctive forces which are always threatening to break through. Freud went so far as to affirm that religion might be regarded 'as a universal obsessional neurosis'.

Religion, therefore, promises protection against unruly impulses from within, by means of ritual observance; and some protection against dangers from without by acquiescing in the restrictive demands of civilization upon the individual's selfish impulses. This renunciation makes possible some degree of solidarity with one's fellow men, and thereby diminishes the sense of helplessness.

In addition, religion promises an after-life. This not only diminishes man's terror in the face of death, but also implies that the dead person will be rewarded with heavenly pleasures to compensate for the earthly pleasures he has had to forego in the interests of civilization.

At the beginning of this chapter, it was noted that Freud regarded civilization as unduly oppressive and provocative of neurosis. His resentment went much further than this; so far, indeed, that one is justified in supposing that his own extreme, obsessional control over his own impulses was burdensome to him. Freud of course recognized that civilization was necessary if man as a species was to survive, but he nevertheless refers to the 'injuries' which civilization inflicts upon the individual. The following quotation is clearly ironically intended, but also reveals what Freud thought of the 'natural' man when unrestrained.

We have spoken of the hostility to civilization which is

produced by the pressure that civilization exercises, the renunciations of instinct which it demands. If one imagines its prohibitions lifted – if, then, one may take any woman one pleases as a sexual object, if one may without hesitation kill one's rival for her love or anyone else who stands in one's way, if, too, one can carry off any of the other man's belongings without asking leave – how splendid, what a string of satisfactions one's life would be! (*SE*, XXI.15).

This sombre picture derives from the fact that psychoanalytic theory is an 'instinct' theory. That is, it is primarily concerned with how the isolated individual finds or fails to find ways of discharging his instinctive impulses. The impression gained from reading Freud is that relationships with other human beings are of value only in so far as they facilitate instinctual satisfaction. There is no conception of friendship or other types of relationship as being valuable in themselves. All are considered 'aim-inhibited' substitutes for sexual relations. No wonder Freud repudiated the Christian commandment 'Thou shalt love thy neighbour as thyself', which he referred to as a precept lacking any point because 'its fulfilment cannot be recommended as reasonable'. As we shall see, modern psychoanalytic theory is much more concerned than was Freud with the quality and type of relationships which the individual makes from birth onwards.

Freud's concept of religion is open to criticism on a number of grounds. First, it is exclusively paternally based. Although Vienna was predominantly a Catholic city, the importance of the Virgin Mary or of any other female goddess is entirely passed over, an omission which was also noted in the discussion of *Totem and Taboo*.

Second, Freud makes no mention of religions like early Buddhism, which appears not to require belief in a god or gods, but which nevertheless prescribes a way of life which many have found profoundly fulfilling.

Third, Freud, as he himself admits, is incapable of understanding ecstatic and mystical experiences, which, for many people, are the origin of 'religious' feelings. When Freud sent a copy of his book dismissing religion, *The Future of an Illusion*, to his friend Romain Rolland, the latter complained that Freud had not comprehended the true source of religious sentiments. Freud wrote:

> This, he says, consists in a peculiar feeling, which he himself is never without, which he finds confirmed by many others, and which he may suppose is present in millions of people. It is a feeling which he would like to call a sensation of 'eternity', a feeling of something limitless, unbounded – as it were, 'oceanic' (*SE*, XXI.64).

Freud rightly characterizes this as

> a feeling of an indissoluble bond, of being one with the external world as a whole (*SE*, XXI.65).

Freud compares this feeling with the height of being in love, in which the lover feels totally at one with his beloved. Freud interprets this as an extreme regression to a very early state; that of the infant at the breast before he has learned to distinguish himself from the mother or the external world. Both being in love and the oceanic feeling are therefore illusions. Indeed, Freud referred to the state of being in love as a kind of madness, as 'the normal prototype of the psychoses'.

Freud partially agrees with Rolland when he admits that the oceanic feeling and the sense of being at one with the universe may become connected with religious sentiments at a later stage, and describes it as

> a first attempt at a religious consolation, as though it were another way of disclaiming the danger which the ego recognizes as threatening it from the external world.
>
> (*SE*, XXI.72)

Although everyone is subject to self-deception and to wish-fulfilling delusions, those who, unlike Freud, have experienced the oceanic feeling, will find themselves dissatisfied with his explanation. The accounts of ecstatic experiences furnished by a variety of people from religious mystics to explorers like

Admiral Byrd suggest that such experiences are the profoundest moments of their existence, and sometimes bring about a permanent alteration in the way in which they perceive themselves and the world. Such experiences do not need to be explained in religious terms, but neither can they be dismissed as totally illusory. Defensive wish-fulfilments usually seem partially inauthentic even to those indulging in them; but the oceanic experience is felt as deeply and inescapably authentic. This is not the context in which to venture an explanation of the oceanic experience. It is enough to state that, if Freud had ever experienced anything of the kind himself, he might have been forced to consider some other interpretation.

Freud ends *The Future of an Illusion* with a device which he constantly employed when discussing topics which he considered particularly controversial: an adversarial debate between himself and an imaginary opponent. Freud proposes that, at some remote date in the future, the intellect will finally assert its primacy and religious belief will thereby be abandoned.

> We may insist as often as we like that man's intellect is powerless in comparison with its instinctual life, and we may be right in this. Nevertheless, there is something peculiar about this weakness. The voice of the intellect is a soft one, but it does not rest till it has gained a hearing. Finally, after a countless succession of rebuffs, it succeeds.
> (*SE*, XXI.53)

Freud equates the intellect with science, although, as indicated earlier, it is impossible to endorse Freud's own view that psycho-analysis is, or could become, strictly scientific. The famous last sentence of Freud's book is:

> No, our science is no illusion. But an illusion it would be to suppose that what science cannot give us we can get elsewhere (*SE*, XXI.56).

It is, perhaps, worth noting that when Freud refers to his imaginary adversary's God as 'your God', the God of conventional religious belief, he opposes what he calls ironically 'our God', Logos, the voice of Reason. Freud's use of this verbal device reveals more about himself than he admitted. Exclusive belief in Reason or Science can be as irrational as belief in God. Certainly, Freud's belief in psycho-analysis went far beyond any evidence of its truth which could possibly be called scientific.

10 Freud as therapist

The Technique of Psycho-Analysis

In Chapter 4, three aspects of psycho-analytic technique were briefly described: free association, the interpretation of dreams, and the evaluation of transference and counter-transference. Freud wrote a number of papers on the technique of psycho-analytic treatment. A summary of what he had to say must be included in even a short book on Freud, for his procedure has influenced nearly every subsequent type of psychotherapy practised in the West. The principles of treatment which Freud enunciated were quite unlike those followed by conventional physicians in the practice of medicine, and must have seemed revolutionary in the period before the First World War when they were formulated. Modern psycho-analysts seldom adhere to all Freud's recommendations; but the general way in which psycho-analysis and other forms of psychotherapy are conducted is still based on Freud's procedure, and remains one of his most enduring legacies.

As early as 1904, Freud laid down certain criteria for the selection of patients as being suitable for psycho-analysis. He required that patients should possess 'a reasonable degree of education and a fairly reliable character'. He refused to take on patients who were psychotic; that is, who were suffering from schizophrenia or from the most severe type of melancholia (depressive illness). As noted earlier, patients suffering from mania or hypomania seldom consult psycho-analysts. Although some psycho-analysts have disregarded Freud's advice in this respect, and have attempted to analyse schizophrenics, the results have been disappointing.

Freud realized that psychotic varieties of mental illness might present as neuroses and not be immediately recognizable as something far more serious. On these grounds, he wisely recommended a trial period of analysis lasting for one or two weeks. He was also cautious in warning against the use of psycho-analysis in cases of *anorexia nervosa* or other dangerous conditions in which immediate removal of symptoms was required.

Freud laid it down that patients 'near or above the age of fifty' were not suitable for psycho-analysis on two grounds. First, he feared that the mass of material which had accumulated during the patient's lifetime would be so great that the treatment might go on indefinitely. This caveat is no longer accepted by modern psycho-analysts, who often treat older patients with success. Freud's other reason for excluding the middle-aged and elderly is more interesting. He says that 'old people are no longer educable', whilst persons under the age of adolescence 'are often exceedingly amenable to influence'. Freud usually claimed that psycho-analysis was a treatment in which direct influence and suggestion played little part. In this passage, he is revealing that suggestion plays a greater role in psycho-analysis than he generally admitted.

In Chapter 4, two reasons were given for requiring the patient to lie supine upon a couch while the psycho-analyst sat out of sight behind him. The first was that this encouraged the flow of free association; the second, Freud's admission that he shrank from being stared at for eight or more hours a day. A third reason was that Freud thought it desirable that the patient should not be aware of the psycho-analyst's changing facial expressions. All three reasons have a certain validity, and most Freudian analysts continue to employ the couch. Analysts belonging to other schools feel that the use of the couch is artificial, and prefer a face-to-face, more equal-seeming encounter, with patient and analyst sitting opposite each other.

Freud recommended that the psycho-analyst take no notes on the grounds that this might interfere with his maintaining an attitude of 'evenly-suspended attention' in which he refused to prejudge which of the patient's utterances were important. Freud pointed out that the significance of what the analyst hears in any particular session may only be established at a later date. The analyst must turn his own unconscious like a receptive organ towards the transmitting unconscious of the patient. He must adjust himself to the patient as a telephone receiver is adjusted to the transmitting microphone (*SE*, XII.113–14).

Any practising psychotherapist will recognize that this is sound advice. One of the commonest mistakes which psychotherapists make is premature interpretation: jumping to wrong conclusions on insufficient evidence.

Convention supposes that psycho-analysts are inhumanly detached; concerned only with the interpretation of the material furnished by the patient, and unmoved by the latter's distress. It has already been noted that Freud, when conducting an analysis, was 'curiously impersonal'. He wrote:

I cannot advise my colleagues too urgently to model themselves during psycho-analytic treatment on the surgeon, who puts aside all his feelings, even his human sympathy, and concentrates his mental forces on the single aim of performing the operation as skilfully as possible. . . . The justification for requiring this emotional coldness in the analyst is that it creates the most advantageous conditions for both parties: for the doctor a desirable protection for his own emotional life and for the patient the largest amount of help that we can give him to-day (*SE*, XII.115).

A certain degree of detachment is undoubtedly required of the analyst. If the analyst identifies himself too closely with the patient, he will abandon objectivity and be unable to see in what way the patient himself is responsible for his own difficulties. On the other hand, if he remains as detached as Freud recommends, there is a danger that he will not be able to understand his patient as a person. Research has established that analysts need to be capable of genuine concern and that warm acceptance on the part of the analyst facilitates personality change. Psycho-analysis and other types of psychotherapy derived from it cannot really be regarded in the same light as surgery, partly because we are no longer as certain as was Freud that we can disinter the origin of every neurotic

symptom as a discrete entity. Modern analysts are more concerned with the patient's personality as a whole, and with the
kind of relationships which he has made throughout his life,
than with repressed infantile sexual phantasy. This concern
demands a different attitude from that recommended by Freud.
Although the analyst must preserve objectivity towards the
patient's behaviour, which he may or may not approve of, he
must also convey what Carl Rogers has aptly called 'uncondi-
tional positive regard'; that is, he must genuinely value the
patient as a person.

In Chapter 4, Freud's acceptance of Jung's requirement that
the analyst should himself be analysed was noted. Freud goes
on to recommend that the analyst should not succumb to the
temptation of talking about his own personality and problems,
as would be natural in social life, when 'one confidence
deserves another'. Freud recommended that:

> The doctor should be opaque to his patients and, like a
> mirror, should show them nothing but what is shown to him.
> (*SE*, XII.118)

Although not every psychotherapist would agree, I think Freud
was entirely right in this requirement. Talking about oneself is
a self-indulgence which should be shunned by the analyst who,
during the analytic hour, must regard himself solely as the
agent of the patient. As Freud points out, self-revelation on the
part of the analyst also leads to insuperable difficulties in interpreting the transference.

Freud warns against didacticism: against recommending
reading matter to the patient, and against trying to direct the
liberated patient into new paths which the analyst thinks he
should follow. Although some psychotherapists use books and
papers as a way of introducing prospective patients to what is
in store for them, Freud was once again perceptive in question-
ing such methods. Reading about psycho-analysis is apt to
provoke intellectual argument at the expense of personal
experience; whilst handing out unsolicited advice is patroniz-
ing, and therefore denigrating to the patient as an autonomous
individual.

Freud advised that most analytic patients should be seen every day except on Sundays and public holidays, although he did say that 'slight cases' or cases 'well advanced' in treatment could be seen less often. He felt that even the interposition of Sunday often had an obscuring effect upon analytic work. The majority of modern psycho-analysts see their patients less often. This is partly because the habit of working on Saturdays has largely disappeared, and partly because only a minority of patients can afford the high fees charged by psycho-analysts if patients have to come on five or six days per week. It is obviously to the analyst's advantage to see more patients less frequently, for he can thereby ask higher fees per session. Freud would not have approved of this modification of his technique.

Freud himself could be generous to those in need, but was decidedly realistic about money. His principle was to allot one particular hour of each working day to each analytic patient and to demand payment for that hour, whether or not the patient made use of it. At first sight, this seems harsh; but Freud defended it on the grounds that, unless required to pay, patients would all too often manifest resistance by failing to appear, and would find manifold excuses for not coming, usually just at the time when some new analytic discovery was imminent.

Freud ostensibly ruled out taking on patients with whom he had any other kind of relationship outside the analytic hour.

> Special difficulties arise when the analyst and his new patient or their families are on terms of friendship or have social ties with one another. The psycho-analyst who is asked to undertake the treatment of the wife or child of a friend must be prepared for it to cost him that friendship, no matter what the outcome of the treatment may be: nevertheless he must make the sacrifice if he cannot find a trustworthy substitute (*SE*, XII.125).

Most psycho-analysts recognize this principle as valid, more especially since analysis of transference became so central a concern of psycho-analytic treatment. But Freud himself often failed to observe his own rules. For example, Freud analysed his own daughter Anna over a period of several years, a flagrant violation of psycho-analytic principles which most psycho-analysts would condemn. It is significant that Anna Freud was the only one of Freud's children to become a psycho-analyst, and that she manifested her continuing devotion to her father by remaining unmarried. During Freud's terminal illness, it was Anna, rather than his wife Martha, who became his nurse.

Freud often failed to obey his own injunctions by talking a good deal himself, sometimes chatting about his family. Hilda Doolittle, the poetess who was a friend of Ezra Pound and at one time married to Richard Aldington, records that, in old age, Freud beat his fist on the head of the couch on which she was lying and said:

> The trouble is—I am an old man—*you do not think it worth your while to love me*.

But those who criticize Freud for breaking the rules of psycho-analysis sometimes appear to forget that it was he who invented them.

Freud's own cases

Freud's case histories have become famous, both as illustrating his own way of conducting psycho-analysis and also as works of literature. A detailed search through Freud's collected works reveals that he mentioned 133 cases in passing, but that there are only six extended accounts of individual patients. These include the case of Judge Schreber, whom Freud never saw, and 'Little Hans', whose father acted as an intermediary. This leaves four cases personally analysed by Freud: 'Dora', who was treated for eleven weeks in 1900; the 'Rat Man', treated for eleven months from October 1907 onwards; and an unnamed female homosexual of 18, whose treatment was discontinued by Freud after 'a short time'. The fourth case is the famous 'Wolf Man', followed up for over sixty years, who died only in 1979.

The case-study of the patient called 'Dora' is judiciously entitled 'Fragment of an Analysis of a Case of Hysteria'. Dora was an 18-year-old girl, the daughter of an unhappily married couple, who were close friends of another unhappily married couple, referred to by Freud as Herr and Frau K. Frau K. was the mistress of Dora's father. Dora had what would now be called a 'crush' on Frau K. Herr K. had made sexual advances to Dora when she was 14, which she violently repudiated. When she became 16, she declared her detestation of Herr K. and said that he had again made advances to her. From this time on, she developed hysterical symptoms of recurrent loss of voice, nervous cough, and fainting spells, together with depression, social withdrawal, and a threat of suicide.

The case of Dora is important because, as Ernest Jones records, it served for years as a model for students of psycho-analysis. As Freud intended, it demonstrates the significance of dreams in psycho-analytic treatment, and bears witness to Freud's ingenuity in interpreting them. It also reveals a good deal which Freud did not intend. At an early point in treatment, Freud made up his mind that Dora, for years, had been in love with Herr K.; a conclusion which was emphatically denied by Dora until the penultimate session of her brief treatment. Freud treated her repeated denials as confirming, rather than negating, his interpretations.

> The 'No' uttered by a patient after a repressed thought has been presented to his conscious perception for the first time does no more than register the existence of a repression and its severity; it acts, as it were, as a gauge of the repression's strength. If this 'No', instead of being regarded as the expression of an impartial judgement (of which, indeed, the patient is incapable), is ignored, and if work is continued, the first evidence soon begins to appear that in such a case 'No' signifies the desired 'Yes' (*SE*, VII.58–9).

Yet, Dora persisted in denying being in love with Herr K. (who, after all, was much older than she was) until she had already decided to terminate her treatment. As others have remarked, Freud overwhelmed her with interpretations until, after that penultimate session, he was able to write:

> And Dora disputed the fact no longer (*SE*, VII.104).

Any reader who studies the case of Dora without prejudice will conclude that, once Freud had made up his mind about a point, he would not take 'No' for an answer, and that he used all his ingenuity and his considerable powers of persuasion to compel his patient to admit that he was right. As already noted, Freud did the same in his writings, especially in those in which he tries to anticipate every objection which an imaginary adversary might raise.

'The Psychogenesis of a Case of Homosexuality in a Woman' underlines the point, now universally recognized by psychoanalysts, that adolescents who are pushed into treatment by their parents seldom do well. Freud recognized this, and also says that this 18-year-old patient

> was not in any way ill (she did not suffer from anything in herself, nor did she complain of her condition).
>
> (*SE*, XVIII.150)

However, six months previously she had made a suicide attempt. Freud had also recognized that the conversion of a homosexual preference into a heterosexual orientation was 'never an easy matter'. Freud warned the parents that their wish to see this change take place in their daughter was unlikely to be fulfilled. Within a short time, it became obvious that the analysis could not succeed. The girl repudiated Freud's interpretations, and, according to his account, manifested a negative transference, based upon her hatred of her father and of men in general. Freud broke off the treatment and recommended that the girl seek help from a woman doctor. His reconstruction of the girl's early sexual development, of what drove her to repudiate men and fall in love with mother-substitutes, and of the events and feelings leading up to her suicidal attempt are of considerable interest. But why, in the face of so many contra-indications to psycho-analysis of which Freud was well aware, did he accept her as a patient? The answer is to be found in the first sentence of the paper.

> Homosexuality in women, which is certainly not less common than in men, although much less glaring, has not only

been ignored by the law, but has also been neglected by psycho-analytic research (*SE*, XVIII.147).

It is clear that Freud took her into treatment in order to remedy this neglect. He must have realized that trying to analyse someone who was not ill and not asking for help was a futile exercise from the patient's point of view, though not from his own. Freud would have agreed that his intellectual curiosity always took precedence over any wish he may have had to act as a therapist. He may well have believed that, because few lesbians presented themselves for treatment, 'using' the patient for research was justified.

The 'Rat Man' is an entirely different proposition. This is one of Freud's most interesting and successful cases. The 'Rat Man' was a lawyer aged 29, who first came to see Freud on 1 October 1907. He complained of obsessional thoughts; that is, of unwanted ideas and phantasies which came into his mind spontaneously, of which he could not rid himself. (Those unfamiliar with such thoughts may recall the common experience of a tune 'running in the head' which cannot be expelled.) The thoughts which assailed Ernst Lanzer (for that was his name) were indeed horrifying. Many consisted of fears that something dreadful would happen to people he was fond of; to his father, or to a lady whom he admired. Freud was astonished to discover that his obsessional fears about his father persisted in spite of the father's actual death some years previously.

But the worst obsessional preoccupation concerned an Eastern punishment of which he had been told while serving in the army. This consisted of tying a pot containing rats to the buttocks of a criminal with the intention that they should bore their way into the man via the anus. Lanzer confessed that the idea had occurred to him that this punishment was being inflicted upon the lady already referred to, and he felt compelled to carry out certain obsessional rituals to ward off this danger.

Freud's long, but necessarily incomplete, account of this case comprises the second half of Volume X of the *Standard*

Edition. It displays Freud at his most brilliant and most convincing. Freud's analysis of obsessional doubts and ambivalence as being ultimately traceable to a conflict between love and hate is persuasive. Freud evidently had a particular empathy with obsessional neurotics, based upon his own obsessional personality. He succeeded in ridding the 'Rat Man' of his tormenting, horrifying thought, and was able to write:

> the treatment, which lasted for about a year, led to the complete restoration of the patient's personality, and to the removal of his inhibitions (*SE*, X.155).

Sceptics may point out that we have no long-term follow-up of Ernst Lanzer. Obsessional neurotics who have been plagued, as he was, with compulsive thoughts and rituals from early childhood seldom lose all their symptoms for ever, and remain vulnerable to relapse at times of stress. As we shall see, this was true of the next case, the 'Wolf Man', who provides us with a long-term follow-up unmatched in the annals of psycho-analysis.

Freud gave his account of the 'Wolf Man' the title 'From the History of an Infantile Neurosis'. The 'Wolf Man' was a wealthy Russian brought up on a large estate. He first consulted Freud in February 1910 and was treated by him until July 1914. Freud notes that at that time he regarded him as cured. The patient records in his memoirs that when he visited Freud in the spring of 1919, after the First World War was over, he was thoroughly satisfied with his own mental and emotional condition and had no thought of seeking further psychoanalysis. However, Freud, on hearing his account of himself, thought differently, and advised a further period of treatment. Freud saw the patient again from November 1919 until February 1920. He reported that

> a piece of the transference which had not hitherto been overcome was successfully dealt with (*SE*, XVII.122).

The 'Wolf Man' suffered from recurrent attacks of depression and from various obsessional symptoms, which, as in the case of the 'Rat Man', manifested themselves in varying degrees of intensity from early childhood onwards. His nickname originates from a fear of wolves dating from his fourth year, and, more particularly, from a nightmare dreamed at about the same period, in which he was terrified by seeing six or seven white wolves sitting on the branches of a walnut tree which stood outside his bedroom window. Freud wrote that he became convinced that behind this dream were concealed the causes of the patient's infantile neurosis. In this context it is impossible to detail the steps which led to Freud's interpretation. Indeed, perhaps wisely, he himself omits many of them from his account. What he concluded 'from the chaos of the dreamer's unconscious memory traces' was that, at the age of 1½, while lying in his cot, he must have witnessed three acts of *coitus a tergo* between his parents. Freud, since the very early days of psycho-analysis, had been convinced that witnessing the 'primal scene' of parental intercourse had a traumatic effect upon young children. This bears out the fact that most of his patients were upper class. In the cramped houses of the poor, such scenes must have been witnessed by young children several times per week; yet Freud more than once hinted that the labouring classes were less liable to neurosis.

Freud was so convinced of the truth of his interpretation that he confidently wrote that his patient's sexual life had been 'splintered up' by this early experience. Yet the 'Wolf Man' himself failed to recollect the incident. Since Freud had forbidden him to be critical, he may have appeared to accept Freud's reconstruction at the time, but he certainly did not do so later. In an interview conducted when he was 87 he revealed:

I never thought much of dream interpretation, you know. In my story, what was explained by dreams? Freud traces everything back to the primal scene which he derives from the dream. But that scene does not occur in the dream. When he interprets the white wolves as nightshirts or something like that, for example, linen sheets or clothes, that's somehow far-fetched, I think. That scene in the dream where the windows open and so on and the wolves are sitting there, and his interpretation, I don't know, these things are miles apart. It's terribly far-fetched.

His account of his analysis with Freud repeatedly emphasizes how impressed he was with Freud's personality, and how he found in him 'a new father'. Freud had

a great deal of personal understanding for me, as he often told me during the treatment, which naturally strengthened my attachment to him.

The 'Wolf Man' reveals that Freud discussed Dostoevsky with him, talked about his son's skiing accident, and did not hesitate to give him direct advice when he thought it appropriate. At the end of the first period of treatment, Freud himself suggested that the 'Wolf Man' give him a present 'so that the feeling of gratitude wouldn't become too strong'. The 'Wolf Man' obliged by adding an Egyptian statuette to Freud's collection. There can be little doubt that the 'Wolf Man's' considerable improvement at this stage in his life was nothing to do with Freud's interpretations of his supposed infantile sexual experiences, and everything to do with the fact that he regarded Freud as an understanding father-figure upon whom he could rely.

When the 'Wolf Man' returned after the war for his second period of analysis, he had lost all his money. Freud treated him free, personally helped him financially, and raised money for him from other sources for a number of years. In 1926 he had another period of analysis with Dr Ruth Mack Brunswick. From then on, he was intermittently treated by Dr Brunswick and by at least three other psycho-analysts. Psychiatrists will recognize a typical history of a chronic obsessional neurotic. He finally died on 7 May 1979, at the age of 92. The series of interviews with him recorded by Karin Obholzer almost to the day of his death disclose that, in his late eighties, he still had problems with his relationships with women, was still subject to bouts of depression, and was still tormented by obsessional thoughts and doubts. Freud's most famous patient is not quite the advertisement for psycho-analysis which Freud might have hoped for after his first encounter with him.

Even when one takes into account the difficulty of presenting psycho-analytic cases without infringing confidentiality, the number of cases treated at any length and discussed in detail by Freud is almost incredibly small. Moreover, only one of the cases displays convincing evidence of substantial improvement. Fisher and Greenberg conclude that:

> Freud never presented any data, in statistical or case study form, that demonstrated that his treatment was of benefit to a significant number of the patients he himself saw.

Why was this? Some might argue that Freud could not produce such data because his treatment did not produce many good results. My own view is that Freud was far more interested in ideas than he was in patients. What he wanted was time and opportunity to present his ideas in so persuasive a way that the whole world would recognize and accept his revolutionary way of looking at human beings. It did not matter whether the cases he chose to present demonstrated the efficacy of psycho-analysis as a treatment. What was important was that the cases selected should support his theories about human nature.

11 Psycho-analysis today

Although Freud himself was primarily concerned with research and psycho-analytic theory rather than with therapy, the reader will wish to know how psycho-analysis stands today, and whether it is considered an effective treatment for neurotic disorders. In spite of the immense amount of research devoted to these questions, they remain extremely difficult to answer. There are a variety of reasons why this should be so.

First, research has demonstrated that psycho-analysts differ so markedly from each other in their treatment aims and expectations, and in how they behave to their patients, that it is not possible to state, even within the Freudian fold, that a defined form of psychotherapy which can be labelled 'psycho-analysis' actually exists. Most studies purporting to examine the outcome of psycho-analysis do not take these variants sufficiently into account. What does seem relatively firmly established is that psycho-analysis, practised in the way which Freud originally laid down, using free association, the couch, and five or six sessions per week, is not more effective in relieving neurotic distress than are less intensive types of analytically orientated psychotherapy. In the 1950s, Eysenck and others tried to demonstrate that psycho-analysis was totally ineffective. This attack had the good effect of stimulating a great deal of research. While it cannot be said that psycho-analysis as practised by Freud is more effective than other forms of psychotherapy derived from it, the consensus is that a person suffering from neurotic problems is certainly more likely to recover if she seeks help from an experienced psychotherapist than if she merely waits for her troubles to pass.

Second, what constitutes cure is very difficult to define. Psycho-analysis, as Freud originally developed it, was primarily concerned with ridding patients of hysterical and obsessional symptoms. In their enthusiasm, the early psycho-analysts and their patients went much further than this in hoping that psycho-analysis would bring about profound changes in personality and character structure. There was much concern with whether 'X' or 'Y' was 'completely analysed', as if this were an achievable result. Freud himself professed no such extravagant aims. Today, most psycho-analysts are less certain than was Freud about defining the 'cause' of a neurosis. When psycho-analysis is effective, and it certainly can be so, it is probable that it works by enabling the patient to make effective use of his psychopathology rather than by abolishing it. Patients presenting themselves for psycho-analysis feel overwhelmed, unable to cope with their problems. Greater understanding of their own strengths and limitations can often be extremely helpful, even if their personality is not fundamentally modified.

In another book I quoted a case of my own which aptly illustrates the difficulty of evaluating the results of any form of psychotherapy. I received a letter from a man whom I had treated rather briefly in a National Health Service setting twenty-five years previously. He wanted me to see his daughter. In his letter he wrote: 'I can quite truthfully say that six months of your patient listening to my woes made a most important contribution to my life style. Although my transvestism was not cured my approach to life and to other people was re-orientated and for that I am most grateful. It is part of my life that I have *never* forgotten.'

Here is an example of a case which might be rated as a dismal failure, since his main symptom, his transvestism, was not abolished. Yet, reading his letter so long after his period of treatment, one is bound to recognize that something important did take place which is directly attributable to that treatment. What seems to have happened is that the limited amount of psychotherapy which I was able to offer made the patient more capable of accepting himself, of coping with his psychopathology rather than letting himself be overwhelmed by it. Such results are more common than is usually admitted; but how they can be scientifically evaluated is an unsolved problem.

In Chapter 1, some aspects of the obsessional personality were outlined. Such personalities are easy to recognize. Although obsessional symptoms can be relieved, as they were in the case of the 'Rat Man', the basic traits which constitute the obsessional personality are not abolished by psycho-analysis. From the 1930s until the 1950s, psycho-analysis was oversold, especially in the United States. More was expected of it than Freud ever claimed it could achieve. Radical change in personality was confidently expected by both patients and psycho-analysts; and the duration of psycho-analytic treatment became more and more extended. I well remember an elderly British psycho-analyst, who appears in the photograph of the Oxford Psycho-Analytic Congress of 1929, telling me about a young man whom he had had in analysis for a number of years. Dr W. was convinced that his patient must have been the victim of a homosexual assault when he was a very small child. If only he could so pierce his defences that he could recall this incident, Dr W. was sure that his patient would recover. Yet any evidence that such an assault had actually occurred was entirely lacking.

That generation of psycho-analysts has passed away. Their modern counterparts are more sceptical. In fact, the case of the 'Wolf Man' aptly prefigures one of the major changes which have come about in psycho-analytic thinking since the death of Freud on 23 September 1939. Freud clearly believed that the patient's apparent cure after his first period of analysis was the result of making conscious his presumed infantile observation of the primal scene. But the 'Wolf Man' thought otherwise. He repudiates Freud's reconstruction of his psychopathology, but constantly reiterates his admiration for Freud.

If you look at everything critically, there isn't much in psycho-analysis that will stand up. Yet it helped me. He was a genius.

The 'Wolf Man' goes on to recall that his father had died before he entered upon treatment with Freud; that his relationship with his father had been poor because has father had preferred his sister; and that it was because of his father's death that he developed a transference to Freud which was so intense that he describes himself as 'worshipping' him.

In other words, the 'Wolf Man' attributes his improvement wholly to his relationship with Freud; to his having discovered a new 'father' who was more tolerant and accepting than his own; one who was prepared to listen to his intimate and sometimes shocking revelations for four years without criticism, revulsion or repudiation of him as a person.

A brief account of transference was given in Chapter 4. Since the 1950s, psycho-analysts have been moving away from Freud's instinct theories to what is unhappily called 'object-relations' theory; that is, towards attributing neurotic problems to early difficulties in interpersonal relationships rather than to blocked instinctual development. Freud originally used the term 'object' as signifying that towards which libido is directed for the purpose of obtaining sexual release. Objects are usually persons; but the term may refer to parts of persons, like the breast, or to substitutes for persons, like fetishes or animals. What has happened is a change of emphasis. Freud was primarily concerned with disinterring repressed infantile sexual phantasies which, he was convinced, were causally implicated in the arrest of the neurotic's libidinal development. Because his sexuality had remained in an infantile state, the neurotic was unable to achieve adult sexual satisfaction, which Freud regarded as the *sine qua non* of mental health. Freud of course realized that deprivation or disturbance in the individual's early relationships with parents were implicated in his arrested development; but his emphasis was upon treating the isolated individual by undoing repression and discovering phantasies or traumatic events dating from earliest childhood, as he professed to do in the case of the 'Wolf Man'. Freud defined the therapeutic aim of psycho-analysis as follows:

Its intention is, indeed, to strengthen the ego, to make it more independent of the super-ego, to widen its field of perception and enlarge its organization, so that it can appropriate fresh portions of the id. Where id was, there ego

111

shall be. It is a work of culture – not unlike the draining of the Zuider Zee (*SE*, XXII.80).

In this statement, there is not a word about improving the patient's interpersonal relationships.

The object-relations school of psycho-analysis is concerned with studying the kind of relationships made by the individual from infancy onward. It particularly emphasizes, as Freud originally did not, the importance of the child's tie with its mother. All psycho-analysts inherit from Freud the conviction that fulfilling sexual relationships are a major component of human health and happiness. But they assume that the ability to achieve satisfying sexual relationships depends upon the prior establishment of secure, loving ties with parents or other care-takers. With Freud, sex comes first, attachment afterwards. With John Bowlby, now established as the most important of the object-relations theorists, secure attachment comes first, sex afterwards.

The consequence of this change in emphasis is that modern psycho-analysts are particularly concerned with analysing transference. The patient who, in early childhood, has been misunderstood, rejected, or ill-treated, will tend to go through life expecting similar treatment from those he encounters. How can he possibly make a satisfactory sexual relationship if, at some level of which he is probably unconscious, he treats every woman as if he was expecting her to criticize or reject him? Moreover, he will exhibit similar attitudes towards the psycho-analyst. The way we were treated in early childhood is bound to condition our expectations of how others will treat us later. The task of the psycho-analyst is to point out such repetitions, and, by continually drawing the patient's attention to the false assumptions which he is making about the analyst, provide a corrective emotional experience, gradually transforming the relationship between them into one in which the patient feels accepted and understood. In severe cases, it may be that the patient never reaches this happy stage; or it may be that he is able to learn to trust the analyst, but is not able to transfer this trust to anyone else. In more favourable instances, the patient will transfer his new-found security to other people in the external world, and, because he is now able to confide in others, become capable of finding love and happiness.

This brief and simplified exposition may seem to be a diversion from the subject of Freud himself. It is not so, because it makes it possible to understand a vital part of Freud's legacy. Anyone who is ignorant of psycho-analysis and who reads the abbreviated account of Freud's description of his cases given in the last chapter might be forgiven for dismissing much of the psycho-analytic theory as nonsense. Apart from the 'Rat Man', the patients show either transient improvement or none at all. Some of Freud's reconstructions are bound to seem far-fetched. Moreover, many people today number among their acquaintances people whom they know to have been 'in analysis' for long periods, but who appear not to have lost all or any of their symptoms. Why do these people persist in pursuing an expensive treatment which appears to do little for them? Why do many psycho-analysts continue to include among their case load a number of patients who do not necessarily lose their symptoms? It is easy to be cynical; to suggest that, provided a patient wants to continue treatment and is prepared to go on paying for it, there is no reason for the psycho-analyst to discharge him. But most psycho-analysts are not short of patients; and it is much more rewarding to treat someone who shows convincing signs of improvement by losing symptoms than it is to continue with a patient who does not.

The situation is further complicated by the fact that the patients who seek psycho-analysis today are rather different from those who consulted Freud. Whereas Freud's patients sought help for clear-cut hysterical or obsessional symptoms, today's patients often consult the analyst for what Szasz has called 'problems in living'; difficulties in inter-personal relationships, or a generalized dissatisfaction with life. This has led to some dispute in psycho-analytic circles. Is the object of psycho-analysis reduction or abolition of neurotic symptoms, or is it the acquisition of self knowledge? Both are laudable aims, and both may be partially realized in the course of psycho-analysis. But is this all that patients are seeking?

What many people underestimate is the revolutionary nature of Freud's procedure, and the effect which this has, irrespective of either insight or the cure of symptoms. Psycho-analysis provides a unique experience which cannot be matched by any other situation in life. What other social circumstance supplies a dedicated listener who, for hour after hour, year after year, will provide a tolerant, understanding, accepting presence; a steadfast friend or substitute parent who never rejects, is never angry, and never punishes? Many psycho-analytic patients embark on treatment because they feel that no one has previously understood them or accepted them; or believe that they dare not reveal their true feelings to anyone because, if they do so, they will be rejected. Psycho-analysis may, at times, be a painful ordeal; but, even if the symptoms do not all disappear, the experience is often so rewarding that psycho-analysts complain that their principal difficulty is in terminating the analysis, not in persuading patients to persist. Freud encountered this difficulty with the 'Wolf Man' during the first period of his treatment, and eventually had to set a date on which the analysis must end.

Freud's technique, which demanded an attitude on the part of the analyst quite unlike that which conventionally obtained between doctor and patient, was, and is, much more important than his theories about infantile sexuality. We have seen that his theory of dreams, on which he so prided himself, cannot withstand critical scrutiny. Freud repeatedly misconceived what was important and what was questionable in his discoveries. His reconstruction of the 'Wolf Man's' infantile sexuality was unconfirmed guesswork. His acceptance of him as a person, his patience, his continuing care over a long period, were underestimated by Freud, yet vital.

In Chapter 4, it was suggested that Freud was reluctant to acknowledge that he became emotionally important to his patients because he wished to be regarded as a skilled technician, an impersonal investigator, a detached scientist. His way of dealing with transference was to treat it wholly as repetition: as a projection upon himself of characteristics which had belonged to the patient's parents and were nothing to do with him in reality. There are two objections to regarding transference only in this light. First, as suggested in Chapter 4, some patients exhibit positive feelings towards the analyst which they have never had before; feelings which they were unable to have towards their parents because the latter were indifferent, hostile or rejecting. Second, Freud was under-estimating the significance of what the long-term nature of his technique actually provided in the here-and-now. He thought that psycho-analysis was bound to be prolonged because of the time required to penetrate the secrets of the patient's infancy. But distressed, alienated people need and value someone whom they perceive as being perceptive, accepting, kind, and continuously concerned with them over a long period, whether or not this acceptance results in the relief of symptoms or in an increase in self-knowledge. In cases in which anything positive is achieved, this is the minimum which can be expected. It is an achievement which should not be underestimated. At best, psycho-analysis and the various forms of individual psychotherapy derived from it can provide insight, relief of distressing symptoms, and an increased capacity for making fruitful interpersonal relationships.

Modern psycho-analysts have recognized the difficulty of defining the exact nature of psycho-analysis. However, an attempt has been made to do so in terms of five basic assumptions. The first is that psycho-analysis is a general psychology which applies to normal human beings as well as to neurotics. Since we all have some neurotic symptoms, the difference between neurotic and normal is one of degree, not of kind.

Secondly, psycho-analysts accept Freud's construct of a 'mental apparatus' which receives stimuli from the external world and which also interacts with the internal physiological systems of the subject's body. Psycho-analysis differs from the kind of psychology employed by experimental psychologists in laboratories in that it is primarily concerned with the individual's subjective experience, and only secondarily with his overt behaviour.

Thirdly, psycho-analysis is concerned with adaptation; with

115

how the subject (or ego) deals with the stimuli impinging upon him both from without and from within. Psycho-analysts do not necessarily accept Freud's Nirvana principle; that is, they think of the organism as striving to reach equilibrium, but this may be a steady state in which conflicting stimuli are balanced one against the other rather than total discharge. Thus, conflict within the mind, conflict between competing stimuli like sex and hunger, or conflict between different parts of the mind like ego and super-ego, are essential aspects of psycho-analytic thinking. So is the notion of the ego using 'defence mechanisms' like repression, projection, denial, and sublimation as ways of coping with the pressures upon it. Psychoanalysis still has rather little to say about 'stimulus hunger': the need to search for stimuli when deprived of them.

Fourthly, psycho-analysts, when considering mental activity, follow Freud in subscribing to determinism. That is, they consider that mental events are subject to the laws of cause and effect. Quite where this leaves the question of free will is unclear. It is certainly possible to argue that neurotic symptoms, like phobias or obsessions, are strictly determined. But their abolition must surely result in the patient having greater freedom to make choices, and choosing is a voluntary act demanding will and intention. While recognizing that everyone has been subjected to genetic and environmental pressures which have restricted power of choice in some respects—for example, sexual orientation—social life would be impossible if we did not assume that we and other people are generally capable of making voluntary decisions and choices. Thomas Szasz, admittedly an unorthodox psycho-analyst, has defined the aim of psycho-analysis as being 'to increase the patient's knowledge of himself and others and hence his freedom of choice in the conduct of his life'.

Fifthly, psycho-analysis assumes that some aspects of mental life are inaccessible to consciousness. Although such mental contents may partially betray themselves in dreams, neurotic symptoms, slips of the tongue, and states of mind encountered in mental illness, most can only be brought into consciousness by the special techniques of recovery and interpretation which are an integral part of the psycho-analytic process. This, perhaps is as far as anyone can go today in trying to define what beliefs and theories are held in common by those calling themselves psycho-analysts.

12 The appeal of psycho-analysis

Freud has graduated from being a 'Modern Master' to being a 'Past Master'. It is now possible to discuss both his achievements and his limitations objectively, without being accused either of swallowing psycho-analysis whole as an uncritical disciple, or else of rejecting it because of personal resistance or lack of insight. Freud has not led us into the promised land, as his staunchest adherents hoped that he would. But Freud's ideas have exerted so powerful an influence that, as Ernest Gellner puts it, psycho-analysis has become 'the dominant idiom for the discussion of the human personality and of human relations'. How and why has this come about?

Freud certainly had many original ideas; but even the most inventive minds are indebted to their predecessors. The thinkers who are credited with causing revolutions in thought are those who appear at times when ideas have been around long enough for a new synthesis to be both possible and generally acceptable. Freud is still sometimes credited with having invented the unconscious; but, as L. L. Whyte demonstrated in *The Unconscious Before Freud*, 'the idea of unconscious mental processes was, in many of its aspects, conceivable around 1700, topical around 1800, and became effective around 1900'. Freud did not invent the idea of the unconscious, but he applied it clinically and made it operational.

L. L. Whyte lists a large number of philosophers, physicians, and others who accepted and promulgated the idea that unconscious processes played an important part in the mental life of man. Those who were most directly influential in shaping Freud's thought include the German physician C. G. Carus (1789–1869), who was a friend of Freud's favourite author Goethe. Carus wrote an influential book, *Psyche*, published in 1846, which began:

The key to the knowledge of the nature of the soul's conscious life lies in the realm of the unconscious. This explains the difficulty, if not the impossibility, of getting a real comprehension of the soul's secret.

Freud's library contained works by Carus, although the latter's name does not appear in the index to Freud's collected works.

Eduard von Hartmann (1842–1906), the author of *Philosophy of the Unconscious*, published in 1869, was another writer whom Freud consulted, Freud acknowledges similarities in their thinking in a footnote added in 1914 to *The Interpretation of Dreams* (*SE*, V.528).

In *An Autobiographical Study*, Freud particularly acknowledges his debt to G. T. Fechner (1801–87), a German psychologist whose ideas influenced Freud's conception that a main function of the mental apparatus was to restore tranquillity by discharging tensions caused by disturbing stimuli. Fechner's ideas are also referred to in *Beyond the Pleasure Principle* (*SE*, XVIII.8–9).

Freud's lack of interest in philosophy was mentioned in Chapter 1 of this book. In an essay entitled 'The Resistances to Psycho-Analysis', first published in 1925, Freud affirmed:

> The philosophers' idea of what is mental was not that of psycho-analysis. The overwhelming majority of philosophers regard as mental only the phenomena of consciousness. For them the world of consciousness coincides with the sphere of what is mental (*SE*, XIX.216).

This curious and inaccurate statement hardly matches what he wrote in the same year in *An Autobiographical Study*:

> Even when I have moved away from observation, I have carefully avoided any contact with philosophy proper. This avoidance has been greatly facilitated by constitutional incapacity. . . . The large extent to which psycho-analysis coincides with the philosophy of Schopenhauer—not only did he assert the dominance of the emotions and the supreme importance of sexuality but he was even aware of the mechanism of repression—is not to be traced to my acquaintance with his

119

teaching. I read Schopenhauer very late in my life. Nietzsche, another philosopher whose guesses and intuitions often agree in the most astonishing way with the laborious findings of psycho-analysis, was for a long time avoided by me on that very account; I was less concerned with the question of priority than with keeping my mind unembarrassed (*SE*, XX.59–60).

A number of writers, including Thomas Mann, Philip Rieff, and Henri Ellenberger, have claimed that Freud must have been more influenced by Schopenhauer and Nietzsche than he acknowledged or perhaps realized. Mann claimed that psycho-analytic concepts were Schopenhauer's ideas translated from metaphysics into psychology. Rieff points out that Freud's attack on religion, *The Future of an Illusion*, is closely similar to Schopenhauer's *Dialogue on Religion*. It was at the suggestion of the maverick analyst Groddeck that Freud adopted the term 'id', which Nietzsche had originally invented. Nietzsche's duality of Dionysian and Apollinian closely resembles Freud's duality of primary process and secondary process. The ideas of Schopenhauer and Nietzsche were widely discussed in intellectual circles. Indeed Freud, while a university student, belonged for five years to a Reading Society of the German Students of Vienna, described by Sulloway as 'a radical pan-German organization in which the views of Schopenhauer, Wagner, and Nietzsche were avidly discussed'.

Every writer concerned with ideas has had the mortifying experience of discovering that what he considered to be an original idea of his own is to be found in the works of another author whom he had forgotten having read. If Freud sometimes claimed priority to which he was not entitled, he is exemplifying his own theories of the wish-fulfilling tendencies of the unconscious rather than engaging in deliberate deception.

Freud is often linked with Darwin and Marx as being one of the three original thinkers who have most altered man's view of himself in the twentieth century. The appetite for books about Freud and his theories still seems to be insatiable, and, even fifty years after his death, bears witness to the pervasiveness of his influence. At the beginning of the twentieth century, when Freud's main theories about the mind were being formulated, Darwin's ideas on evolution and the descent of man had recently won acceptance. Darwin, by demonstrating that man was not a special creation, but simply the most highly evolved primate, had paved the way for a psychology which was not based upon the philosophy of mind, or upon perception, or upon conditioned reflexes, or upon man's spiritual qualities, but one which was rooted in his kinship with animals. The time was ripe for a psychology based upon 'instinct'; that is, upon the basic biological forces or 'drives' motivating the behaviour of both man and animals, of which sex is certainly one of the most important.

Darwin had even concluded that language, a distinctive form of social interaction peculiar to man, had originated from expressive cries emitted during courtship, gradually evolving into words capable of defining more and more complex emotions. As Frank Sulloway has pointed out in his study *Freud, Biologist of the Mind*, it was Darwin who 'singled out the biological importance of the instincts for survival and for reproduction, laid before the medical community a dynamic and dualist paradigm of instinct that seemed to encompass the whole of organic behaviour'.

Darwin had shaken man's self-esteem by demonstrating his kinship with other animals. Freud shattered it still further by asserting that man was far less a master in his own mental house than he had supposed. The voice of the intellect might be persistent as well as soft, but men were far more governed by emotion and irrationality than they commonly realized; and Freud affirmed that even man's loftiest achievements in the arts and philosophy were sublimations of primitive instinct.

Darwin's portrayal of man was 'reductive', in that he not only dispelled the notion of man as a special creation in God's image, but also tended to reduce highly complex behaviour to simple biological origins. Freud was attempting to do exactly the same thing; and one reason why psycho-analysis spread so widely was that it appeared to be in line with the new biology. Freud's debt to Darwin was certainly considerable, as he himself admitted.

121

Freud also belonged to the era in which physicists were beginning to discern the structure of matter. The electron was discovered in the 1890s. Soon, a multiplicity of subatomic particles made their appearance. It is hardly fanciful to say that, at the beginning of the century, scientific understanding was equated with reducing structures, including that of the mind, to their elementary constituents. This may explain why some of the deficiencies of psycho-analytic theory were overlooked or dismissed. As indicated earlier, Freud's attempt to explain art and religion in terms of sublimated infantile sexuality and escapist phantasy is profoundly unsatisfactory. Freud's purely reductive stance omits any consideration of synthesis, of the need to make new wholes out of apparently disparate entities, of Gestalt psychology, or of what Koestler later called 'bisociation'. Freud also omitted to study cognitive development, or to define social development in any other terms than those of psychosexual development within the nuclear family. He only felt that he was on solid ground when he had succeeded in reducing the mental to the physical, 'the indispensable organic foundation' upon which he insisted.

This uncompromising reductionism has a considerable emotional appeal. Any system of thought which is called 'scientific' and which promises a new understanding of human nature by getting down to a few basic essentials, is likely to appeal to those people who pride themselves on being hard-headed realists, undeceived by talk of altruism, self-sacrifice, disinterested love, or clap-trap about morality. Freud was expert at reducing all human striving to the lowest common denominator. It is not inappropriate to point out that this technique is also characteristic of Jewish humour. Those who subscribe to psycho-analysis as an all-embracing system of explaining human behaviour not only tend to pride themselves on being aggressively realistic and upon possessing esoteric knowledge denied to others, but also commonly use this knowledge in a manner reminiscent of the 'one-upmanship' techniques catalogued by Stephen Potter. 'I understand everything better than you do; you are neurotic, but I really know.' Carried to extremes, this results in the 'character assassination' referred to earlier in connection with Freud and Bullitt's biography of Woodrow Wilson.

Psycho-analysis has often been referred to as a religion, partly because of the intensity of the disputes within the movement which so often led to rebels leaving it and setting up rival schools, or splinter groups, in a manner reminiscent of religious sects. Freud always denied that psycho-analysis provided a *Weltanschauung* of its own, and devoted the last of his *New Introductory Lectures on Psycho-Analysis* to claiming that psycho-analysis did not depart from the criteria of science, and therefore looked at the world through scientific eyes. Yet, virtually everyone except a few fundamentalist Freudians agrees that psycho-analysis is very far from being a science, since its theories are not open to refutation and cannot be used for prediction. But psycho-analysis has certainly provided a belief system. In his last introductory lecture, Freud wrote that Marxism

> has acquired the energy and the self-contained and exclusive character of a *Weltanschauung*, but at the same time an uncanny likeness to what it is fighting against. . . . Any critical examination of Marxist theory is forbidden, doubts of its correctness are punished in the same way as heresy was punished by the Catholic Church (*SE*, XXII.180).

Exactly the same was true of psycho-analysis in its early days, although its heretics, Adler, Stekel, Jung, Rank, and many others, were not subjected to torture or execution, but only to character assassination by being labelled neurotic or psychotic. Some of the language used to describe such heretics is almost unbelievably intemperate. Today, there is a truce between the previously warring factions of the British Psycho-Analytical Society; but it is an armed truce, and, in private, psycho-analysts belonging to one of the three groups into which the Society is divided are apt to make scathing remarks about other psycho-analysts who are not of their persuasion. The delusion that one group rather than another is the guardian of psycho-analytic 'truth' is still regrettably evident.

As indicated earlier, Freud was inclined to derive intellectual curiosity and a passion for knowledge from infantile sexual researches, rather than accepting that man might possess a propensity for exploratory behaviour analogous to that shown by many other species. Perhaps this interpretation derived from his own childhood memory of penetrating his parents' bedroom out of curiosity, and of being ordered out by an angry father. Freud himself certainly possessed a huge appetite for knowledge, and a powerful drive to make sense out of the bewildering maze of mental phenomena. Freud attacked philosophy on the grounds that, unlike science, it attempted to present a picture of the universe which was too coherent, too lacking in gaps. Moreover, he affirmed, philosophy was of interest only to a few intellectuals, and was scarcely intelligible to anyone else. Yet Freud himself did not confine himself to an explanation of neurotic symptoms. As we have seen, from the earliest days of psycho-analysis onwards, he strove to create a coherent system of ideas which would not only explain all forms of mental illness, but also religion, art, literature, humour, the descent of man, and man's social organizations. The appeal of psycho-analysis, the fact that it became a movement rather than remaining as a type of medical treatment for neurosis, surely derives from its claim to explain so much. Psycho-analysis lacks many of the features usually associated with religion, but, in a secular age, in which those who could not subscribe to the old faiths often felt rootless and insecure, psycho-analysis offered an explanatory system which was eagerly embraced as a substitute.

It also offered membership of an esoteric brotherhood which consisted of those who had been analysed, if not by Freud himself, by one of his disciples, or by one of the disciples of his disciples. A great deal of psycho-analytic wisdom seems to have depended upon oral transmission rather than upon writings. Psycho-analysis, at least in its earlier days, seemed to proffer a secular form of salvation. Moreover, if patients did not get better, or if trainees did not whole-heartedly embrace all the principles which Freud had laid down, psycho-analysts were often able to convince them that it was their fault, not the fault of the system. This is typical of all esoteric systems of belief, from the Plymouth Brethen to the Moonies.

The widespread adoption of psycho-analysis was fostered by Freud's marvellously persuasive style of writing. Even when the ideas he is advancing do not stand up to scrutiny, it is still a pleasure to read him, even in translation. I cannot think of any other psycho-analytic writer who is his equal, although I can think of many who appear to be wilfully obscure. Jacques Lacan, the revolutionary French psycho-analyst who attempted to link psycho-analysis with linguistics, is the prime example. But when an author combines elegance of style, persuasiveness, and an absolute conviction of his own rightness, it is hard to resist him. Freud is often praised by Freudians for his apparent flexibility; for his willingness to alter his theories as psycho-analysis grew and developed. But the history of the psycho-analytic movement bears witness to Freud's intolerance of opposition. Although he himself might alter or develop his theories, virtually no one else was allowed to do so, with the possible exception of members of his supposedly loyal Committee, a small inner circle which included Karl Abraham and Ernest Jones. In his certainty of his own rightness, Freud resembled one of his severest critics, the philosopher of science, Karl Popper. It is interesting that Popper uses the same adversarial technique as did Freud to undermine his opponents.

Freud's confidence that his basic ideas were correct added considerably to his power to attract a large following, although it is out of keeping with a truly scientific stance. The majority of human beings are only too ready to follow a leader who professes complete conviction, since such a course relieves them from the anxiety inseparable from uncertainty, and from the effort of thinking for themselves. It is not difficult to point to recent political examples of leaders exhibiting single-minded confidence of a comparable kind, however narrowly based. As Norman Cohn demonstrated in *The Pursuit of the Millennium*, utter conviction lends charisma even to figures much less original and impressive than Freud.

Freudian theory made Western man suspicious of conduct previously regarded as virtuous, often with unfortunate consequences. In 1900 the person who displayed altruism and self-sacrifice would simply have been regarded as 'good'. Since Freud, people are inclined to suspect unselfishness as masochistic self-punishment, and altruism as concealing a wish to patronize. Unselfishness and generosity are still virtues; but Freud has made it easier for those who do not wish to cultivate these virtues to justify their avoidance of them. Celibacy used to be admired. Now it is invariably interpreted as concealing perversion or as an ignominious flight from sex, rather than as self-control or evidence of spiritual excellence. The Victorians were more, not less, tolerant of homosexual feelings, if not of homosexual practices, than we are. Tennyson's *In Memoriam*, his long lament over the death of his beloved friend Arthur Hallam, could not be published today except by a poet who had 'come out'; that is, who was openly and avowedly homosexual. Those who are certainly predominantly heterosexual, as was Tennyson, seem to be allowed less latitude than formerly in expressing passionate friendship involving their own sex. As Freud asserted that everyone is bisexual at some level, this seems odd. However, psychoanalysis has, on the whole, increased both understanding and tolerance for those who do not follow conventional sexual patterns. Sex may not be quite the prime mover which Freud thought it to be; but we do owe him a considerable debt for having lifted the covers of Victorian prudery and made sex into a subject which can be openly and seriously discussed.

Freudian theory has also increased tolerance in other respects. Because of Freud's insistence that the seeds of neurosis are sown in early childhood, we pay more attention to our children's emotional needs, and are, perhaps, more inclined to try and understand them rather than to punish them when they behave antisocially. The same is true of our attitudes to criminals. Although we are still almost totally ineffective at dealing with habitual criminals, there is a greater realization that savage punishments neither deter nor reform, and a greater inclination to perceive that antisocial conduct may reflect alienation from society or feelings of despair rather than innate wickedness.

Although psycho-analysis has not proved more effective than other forms of psychotherapy in the treatment of neurosis, Freud's technique of listening to distressed people over long periods has had a strikingly beneficial effect upon all forms of psychotherapy derived from psycho-analysis. As indicated earlier, even those who do not lose all their symptoms usually gain increased self-understanding and a sense of being accepted as persons which they may never have previously experienced. Freud's passion for investigation and his lack of therapeutic enthusiasm led, ironically, to his most important legacy. Anyone can give 'good advice' to people in distress. It was Freud who taught us how to listen.

Freud's excursions into fields outside the consulting room seem for the most part ill-judged. It requires a very dedicated Freudian to accept Freud's ideas about religion, anthropology, or art. It may even be that the status of psycho-analysis would be higher if Freud had not used his theories to try and explain so much in addition to neurosis, perversion, and psychosis. But perhaps it was unavoidable, given that he was determined to construct a psychology which applied as much to the normal person as it did to the neurotic. It is worth repeating Breuer's judgement, which was quoted in Chapter 1:

> Freud is a man given to absolute and exclusive formulations: this is a psychical need which, in my opinion, leads to excessive generalization.

What one can say with conviction is that, even if every idea which Freud put forward could be proven wrong, we should still be greatly in his debt. Although psycho-analysis is not a science in the same category as the 'hard' sciences of physics and chemistry, the history of ideas demonstrates that, in so far as our understanding of ourselves and the world can be said to increase, it progresses in the way that Popper claims for science; that is, by refutation of existing hypotheses. Freud was enormously inventive and ingenious. He did cause a revolution in the way we think. He produced a considerable number of hypotheses which, even when wrong, deserve serious consideration and detailed refutation. Eysenck dismisses psycho-analysis as unworthy of attention because it is unscientific. Medawar called it a 'stupendous intellectual confidence trick'. But psycho-analysis has had such an inescapable influence upon our thinking that it must resonate with something deep within us. At the very least, psycho-analysis deserves informed critical examination rather than simple dismissal. Perhaps the 'Wolf Man' was right when he said:

> Freud was a genius, there's no denying it. All those ideas that he combined in a system. . . . Even though much isn't true, it was a splendid achievement.

Further reading

Freud, Sigmund, *The Standard Edition of the Complete Psychological Works of Sigmund Freud*, translated from the German under the general editorship of James Strachey, in collaboration with Anna Freud, assisted by Alix Strachey and Alan Tyson, 24 vols. (London, 1953–74). Referred to throughout this book as *SE* followed by vol. no. and page: e.g. (*SE*, V.96).

Clark, Ronald W., *Freud: The Man and the Cause* (London, 1980). One of the three major biographies published in English. Workmanlike, thorough, readable.

Farrell, B. A., *The Standing of Psycho-Analysis* (Oxford, 1981). An appraisal of psycho-analysis by a philosopher who does not let his knowledge of, and sympathy with, the subject impair his critical stance.

Fisher, Seymour, and Greenberg, Roger P., *The Scientific Credibility of Freud's Theories and Therapy* (New York, 1977). A comprehensive review of all the important objective research into psycho-analytic theory and treatment undertaken before 1977. An indispensable work of reference.

Gay, Peter, *Freud: A Life for Our Time* (London, 1988). The most recent biography of Freud by a distinguished cultural historian. Gay is also a graduate of the Western New England Institute of Psychoanalysis and thus understands the subject from the inside.

Gellner, Ernest, *The Psychoanalytic Movement* (London, 1985). A malicious, sometimes unfair, but invariably funny attack upon psycho-analysis which seeks to explain the social needs and climate which fostered the acceptance of psycho-analysis and turned it from a medical treatment into a movement.

Grosskurth, Phyllis, *The Secret Ring* (New York, 1991). An excellent account of Freud's *Secret Committee* of six supposedly faithful disciples. Their intrigues and infidelities point to psycho-analysis as a faith rather than a scientific enterprise.

Horden, Peregrine, ed., *Freud and the Humanities* (London, 1985). A collection of papers originally given as the Chichele Lectures during 1984 under the auspices of All Souls College, Oxford. The contributors include the art historian Ernst Gombrich, the Regius Professor of Greek at Oxford, Hugh Lloyd-Jones, and the late Richard Ellmann, biographer of James Joyce and Oscar Wilde.

Jones, Ernest, *Sigmund Freud: Life and Work*, 3 vols. (London, 1953–7). A classical biography by Freud's closest British adherent. Although Jones is too uncritical a disciple, and although subsequent biographies have uncovered more facts, this still remains indispensable.

Kline, Paul, *Fact and Fantasy in Freudian Theory* (London, 1972). Another valuable account of objective research into Freud's theories which supplements Fisher and Greenberg's book in a number of areas.

Masson, Jeffrey M., tr. and ed., *The Complete Letters of Sigmund Freud to Wilhelm Fliess, 1887–1904* (Cambridge, Mass. and London, 1985). These letters are the most important source book for understanding the development of psycho-analysis in its early stages. This is the first complete edition in English, since many of the letters (which were never intended for publication) were previously withheld or heavily censored by the guardians of the Freud archives.

McGuire, William, ed., *The Freud/Jung Letters* (London, 1974). A scrupulously edited, fascinating collection of letters which tell the sad story of how two original thinkers discovered each other, became deeply involved, both intellectually and emotionally, and then became gradually estranged, finally parting in bitterness.

Rieff, Philip, *Freud: The Mind of the Moralist* (London, 1960). An extremely intelligent American appraisal of Freud, with especial emphasis on Freud's place in the history of ideas. Rieff calls psycho-analysis 'the last great formulation of nineteenth-century secularism'.

Roazen, Paul, *Freud and His Followers* (New York, 1975).

Between 1964 and 1967, Roazen succeeded in interviewing over seventy people who had known Freud personally. Roazen has a nose for scandal and an unrivalled knowledge of many of those who were closest to Freud, as well as being a scholarly chronicler of the psycho-analytic movement. There is a good deal of material here which cannot be found elsewhere, presented in highly readable form.

Rycroft, Charles, *A Critical Dictionary of Psychoanalysis*. Second Edition (London, 1995). Anyone puzzled by psycho-analytic terminology, as most of us sometimes are, will find Rycroft's book an invaluable source of accurate definitions which elegantly explain even the most obscure concepts.

Sulloway, Frank J., *Freud: Biologist of the Mind* (New York, 1979). A long, detailed, and important account of the biological origins of Freud's theories. Sulloway places Freud in the context of the history of ideas in unique fashion, and demolishes the myth that Freud was an isolated, heroic figure whose ideas were universally repudiated. Every modern Freudian scholar acknowledges a debt to Sulloway.

Webster, Richard, *Why Freud Was Wrong* (London, 1995). A controversial, original, brilliant, and learned book which contends that Freud became a kind of Messiah, and that psychoanalysis is really a disguised continuation of Judaeo-Christian religious transition. An indispensable modern critique of psychoanalysis.

Whyte, Lancelot Law, *The Unconscious Before Freud* (London, 1962). Essential reading for anyone interested in the history of ideas. Whyte demonstrates that Freud's theories were the culmination of a cultural process extending over several centuries, and that many of his 'discoveries' had been anticipated by previous thinkers.

Wollheim, Richard, *Sigmund Freud* (London, 1971). Freud as a 'Modern Master'. A valuable exposition of Freud's theories of the mind by a distinguished philosopher. But Professor Wollheim is too convinced a Freudian to be entirely objective. Perhaps this is why there is little discussion of Freud's incursions into art, and an uncritical acceptance of Freud as a therapist.

Index